The Lion of Vienna

Dedication . . .

To the people of Bolton. Without you, none of this would have been possible.

'The Lion of Vienna'

* * *

NAT LOFTHOUSE

50 years a legend

* * *

As told to

ANDREW COLLOMOSSE

Foreword by Tom Finney

SPORTSPRINT PUBLISHING
EDINBURGH

John Donald Publishers Ltd.,
138 St. Stephen Street, Edinburgh EH3 5AA.

ISBN 0 85976 284 X

Our thanks to *The Bolton Evening News* for generous help in providing access to their photographic library and in supplying pictures for this book.

Phototypeset by Beecee Typesetting Services
Printed in Great Britain by Bell & Bain Ltd., Glasgow

Foreword

I FIRST met Nat Lofthouse when he was just 17. Needless to say, he was wearing the white shirt of Bolton Wanderers. It was during the War. I had signed as a part-timer with Preston before I was called up but Deepdale was being used as a Prisoner of War camp . . . so there wasn't much chance of getting a game there!

I was stationed down south at Tidworth and if I was coming home on leave I would try to fix myself up with a game in Lancashire. That's how I came to be playing alongside Nat for Bolton against Burnley. He scored twice and it was obvious even then that he was going to be an outstanding player.

Our careers have run on parallel lines ever since. We made our League debuts in 1946, we both played over 400 League games for one club and we both finished around the same time, the early sixties. We played for England together many times. We have remained great pals.

I have nothing but happy memories of playing with and against Nat. We had some rare tussles against Bolton at Burnden Park and at Deepdale. Nat was hard but he was fair. He would always be there with a handshake at the final whistle.

And in the England team he was a great colleague, the kind of man you always wanted to have on your side. Nat would never hide. If you were in trouble you would always look for him. And he would be there to help you out. No wonder they christened him The Lion of Vienna. No more lionhearted player ever wore an England shirt.

Nat is the King of Bolton. It is a marvellous achievement to spend 50 years with one club, and Bolton Wanderers' decision to give him a testimonial is an indication of how the people of Bolton feel about him nearly 30 years after he finished playing.

But despite all the acclaim, Nat has never changed. He is still the level-headed, down to earth Lancastrian I first met all those years ago. He says what he thinks. You always know exactly where you stand with him. I am proud to be his friend.

Tom Finney

Preface

IT is a cold, grey February day in Bolton. The year? 1933. A small boy scampers down Manchester Road, leaping over the puddles as he goes. Above him tower the stands of Burnden Park, home of Bolton Wanderers Football Club. Today they are at home to Manchester City in the fifth round of the F.A. Cup, a fixture that has attracted nearly 70,000 people into the famous ground. The boy should be at school. Like many others, he has played truant to come and watch his idols. A policeman indulgently looks the other way as the boy shins up a drainpipe at the back of the ground. From his perch, high above the terraces, the boy watches, entranced. One day, he dreams, I will play here. I will wear the white shirt of the Wanderers. Nat Lofthouse's lifelong love affair with his hometown club has begun.

Contents

		Page
	Foreword by Tom Finney	v
	Preface	vii
1.	*The Happy Wanderer*	1
2.	*Opportunity Knocks*	4
3.	*Wembley Wonderland*	9
4.	*The Cup of Tears*	12
5.	*The Cup That Cheers*	16
6.	*England My England*	23
7.	*The Lion of Vienna*	31
8.	*A Pain in Spain*	35
9.	*Flower of Scotland*	39
10.	*Let's Call It Quits*	43
11.	*Management Man*	48
12.	*Thrown a Lifeline*	56
13.	*Name, Please!*	62
14.	*The Show Must Go On*	67
15.	*1966 And All That*	72
16.	*My Italian Job*	79
17.	*A Family Affair*	84
18.	*Hillsborough*	88
19.	*Fifty Not Out*	93
	Index	95

CHAPTER ONE

The Happy Wanderer

ALL I ever wanted to do was play football. I was hopeless at my studies. If I finished three from the bottom I thought I was doing well. It was football first and last. That's been the story of my life.

Funnily enough, though, the first proper game I can remember I played in goal . . . and we lost 7-1. The first-choice goalkeeper had dropped out, so they gave me the job instead. And that wasn't the only hiding I got that day. My mother had just bought me a pair of new shoes and you can imagine the reception when I got home.

My grandmother came to the rescue at home with another pair of shoes and the games master came to my rescue by picking me at centre-forward from then on. That was at Brandwood Street School, Bolton, back in 1930 when I was five years old.

My father, Richard, was never too interested in football . . . at least not until I signed for Wanderers. He used to come and watch me then. But both he and mother Sarah Jane followed my progress. They wanted to know who I was playing against, if we'd won and so on. And they always made sure I had the right kit . . . although I always used to stuff newspapers down my socks to make shin pads.

My dad was a coalbagger. And with my mum and three brothers to support on £2 10 shillings a week he didn't have a lot to spare to watch football. My brothers, Edward, Dick and Tom, were all keen players, though, and Dick and Tom played for the Bolton Co-Op team. They were great days at school, although we didn't realise it at the time. I suppose everyone says that, don't they? When we weren't playing at school we'd be playing at home in the street with coats as goalposts. We could never afford a proper football, of course, so whoever had the nearest thing was the most important kid around.

After primary school I went to Castle Hill School at the age of 10. I was still football mad. Tommy Lawton, one of the greatest centre-forwards this country has produced, went to the same school. So I had someone to aim at. We used to have two inter-schools competitions called the Morris Shield and the Stanley Shield. There were some cracking games. It was at Castle Hill that I first got chosen for the Bolton schools team when I was 12. We'd play all the other towns round and about us.

In one match against Bury Schools I scored seven goals . . . and a friend of my Dad's bought me a bike. He was called Bert Cole. He had first spotted me as an eleven-year-old in the Castle Hill team. Sometimes on a Sunday morning he would go with me and my brother Tom, who was in the same school team, and make us practise heading and shooting.

I always played up front even then. I suppose I didn't have the brain to be an inside forward or a wing-half. We had boys who could win the ball, boys who could use it, boys who could beat a man and cross it . . . and me in the middle. Scoring was always important to me.

I remember one Saturday I met Tommy Lawton at the bus stop. He used to live in Tonge Moor, the same area as us. I was off to play for the town team and Tommy was catching the bus to Burnley. That's where he started his career. I'll always remember what he said to me that day. 'Nat,' he said. 'No matter how you play, always try to score. That's the important thing.' I always did, too. I asked him for his autograph that day and he gave it to me. It's something I'll always remember.

When I wasn't playing I'd go down to Burnden. They had a good team in those days; they were a big club. There were anything up to nine Lancashire teams in the First Division then. We'd go and watch Wanderers playing sides like Blackpool, Blackburn, Burnley, Preston as well as United, City, Liverpool and Everton. They were all wary of Bolton.

It was threepence to go in as a schoolboy and stand on the embankment. Sixpence in the paddock and one and threepence for a seat. Ray Westwood was the man we all went to see. Inside left, played for England. Good player. He could run at defenders, take people on. He was the idol of Bolton. I used to imagine I was him.

I remember going down to the Odeon cinema one Friday night. I'd be about nine years old, I suppose. Westwood had been unfit all week and was doubtful for the match next day. All of a sudden they flashed on to the screen: 'Westwood will play at Burnden tomorrow.' A huge roar went up inside that cinema. That was the way they used to let people know that kind of thing . . . and make sure they got a good crowd next day. But Westwood wasn't the only great player in that side.

There was the half-back line of Harry Goslin, Jack Atkinson and George Taylor. And men like George Hunt, Tommy Woodward, Teddy Rodwell and Jimmy Currier. All fine players.

All this time I was still playing for Castle Hill and the Bolton Schools team. I wasn't aware of any interest from Wanderers or any other clubs. There were no scouts knocking on the door late at night or anything dramatic like that! Whenever we played there would be a few people standing on the touchline but we always assumed they were parents, teachers, friends and so on. Maybe some of them were scouts but we were too busy playing football to notice.

The first inkling I had was when the Mayor of Bolton, Councillor Jim Entwhistle, came to Castle Hill to present the prizes. He was on the board at Burnden and he must have been told about me because he asked me if I would like to play for Wanderers. He didn't have to ask again. So, at the age of 14, I signed for Wanderers. The date: September 4, 1939. The day after the outbreak of World War Two.

Westwood, Taylor, Goslin and the rest went off to War leaving us behind. I went to work at Peter Caffery and Sons, a firm who made reeds for the mills. I was there for about three and a half years before I went down the pit as one of the Bevin Boys. Mossley Colliery.

That was one of the best things that ever happened to me. I was still playing all the football I could. I was still pretty fit. But working down there took off a lot of puppy fat, hardened me up. And it was tough work, too. Those guys do work hard. I've a lot of time for miners; they're the best guys in the world. They were brilliant to me. I thought nothing of going down the pit at five or six in the morning and then coming up at 11 o'clock and setting off to play football at somewhere like Tranmere.

They were good days . . . and they made me all the more determined to be a footballer rather than go back down the pit and work for a living. Yes, work for a living. I never thought being a footballer was working. It was a privilege. I was being paid to do something I loved, something every-one else wanted to do.

It seemed too good to be true.

CHAPTER TWO

Opportunity Knocks

SO there I was, newly signed for Wanderers; my childhood dreams had come true. But I was all dressed up with nowhere to go. For football as we knew it ended when War broke out and the senior players at Burnden Park went off to fight. We had a professional staff of 35 when the War started. Thirty-two of them joined up. In fact, 15 men had joined the Territorial Army in May, 1939, so when War broke out in September, most of them were called up immediately. Stan Hanson, Danny Winter, George Catterall, Harry Goslin, Jack Hurst, Ernie Forrest, Jack Ithell, Albert Geldard, Tommy Sinclair, Jack Roberts, Don Howe and Ray Westwood joined the Bolton Artillery and were posted overseas.

They went on to become a sort of Wartime Wanderers. They played together in places like Cairo and Baghdad and all over Italy during the Italian campaign. It was in Italy that poor Harry Goslin was killed in action. For those of us left behind, there was wartime football. The season started with a League competition on a regional basis, then, later in the season, a Cup. There was a northern zone and a southern zone, with a play-off between the two winners.

I made my Wanderers debut in a Wartime League game against Bury in March 1941. I was 15 years old. I scored twice. In those days you never really knew who would be playing alongside you as players from other clubs who were stationed nearby could turn out as guests. I met some important people!

One Saturday I was standing on Bolton station when Bill Shankly strolled up and said he was playing for Wanderers. He was stationed at Warton, just outside Blackpool. He played three games for us in the 1943-44 season.

Cliff Chadwick, the Middlesbrough player, was also stationed there and he turned out for us a lot over the years. Players all over the country would write to clubs around their stations, say they were available and wait for the call. I think they were paid about £2 a time.

That's how I first came to play alongside Tom Finney. He played for Wanderers against Burnley in 1942. Just the one match — but I was to share countless great moments with him down the years.

Of course not all the pre-War Wanderers were away all the time. Harry Goslin, George Taylor, Jack Atkinson, Stan Hanson, Don Howe, Jack Ithell, Danny Winter and Ray Westwood appeared at one time or another. George Hunt played fairly regularly throughout the War years. But for the most part it was local players and youngsters like me who formed the backbone of the team week in and week out. Men like Ralph Banks, Matt Barass and Willie Moir were making their way into the side with me. Men with whom I would share some of my happiest days.

And if the players turned up on a Saturday not knowing who would be in the side, how do you think the fans felt? They'd arrive at Burnden to discover Finney was in the side . . . or Shankly. There were no programmes. The team names would be carried around the ground on a big blackboard. If you were down at the front, you could read it and pass the word back. Of course, on wet days, the rain rubbed it out before the man carrying the board could get round the pitch. But it didn't matter. People were just glad to be watching football.

But it wasn't some sort of Sunday School Combination. Don't get that idea. These were big games played in front of big crowds. It was important. Take the year 1945, my first real taste of Cup glory. We started the League Cup trail against our neighbours Accrington Stanley, who were to drop out of the League in the fifties. They were two-leg matches and we won that first round 4-0.

In the next round we drew Blackpool. That was harder but we got through 5-3 to earn a third-round tie against Newcastle United. This one went to extra-time in the second leg before we scrambled through 5-4 on aggregate. We beat Wolves 4-3 in the semi-final and went on to face Manchester United in the northern final. They were two thrillers but we ran out winners 3-2. Chelsea won the southern section so it was down to Stamford Bridge for the Cup Final. Sudden death . . . not two legs. We were 1-0 down at half-time but George Hunt equalised and then we were awarded a penalty late on. Lol Hamlett scored. We had won the last wartime Cup. A good way to go out.

Since making my debut on that March day in 1941, I had played in 139 games and scored 100 goals. In 1939, I'd signed up for Wanderers at

14, a schoolboy. Seven years and a World War later I was a regular first teamer. I wouldn't dispute for a minute how lucky I was. If I'd signed for Wanderers under normal circumstances in peacetime, there's no way I would have played over 100 games between 1941 and 1946. I would have been making my way up the ladder in the juniors and the reserves. Instead I learned my trade in the senior side.

And when the war ended, some of the men who came back were maybe getting a wee bit over the hill. They hadn't been playing regular football; I had. It was a chance I was lucky to get. I was young, eager and raring to go. And I had George Taylor.

If I had to name one man who had a greater influence on my career than anyone else, I would have to say George Taylor. He was a regular in the side before the War and took up where he left off afterwards, a senior member of the side. He was one of those players who never have a bad game. Always there, week in and week out. Utterly dependable. If the manager wanted him to mark an opponent out of the game he would do so. If he was told to restrict himself to a particular role, he would do that. You could rely on George.

And he was a good man. Didn't drink or smoke. He was honest and straightforward and a source of inspiration to the young players on and off the field. One of the best things they ever did at Burnden Park was make George Taylor coach when he retired. He had the gift of making people play for him. He had a good relationship with the manager, Bill Ridding.

In those days, most clubs had a secretary-manager, that was Bill, and a coach, George. Bill left George to get on with what he was good at . . . coaching and handling people. He was our coach in both the 1953 and 1958 Cup Finals. He also helped the reserves and youngsters and did some scouting, too. He was mainly responsible for getting the 1958 team together. He was the complete clubman. He preached that the club was always bigger than the individual. We were playing for the club, the town, the people of Bolton.

I'll give you a good example of what I mean. I won my first England cap against Yugoslavia at Highbury in 1950. We drew two apiece and I scored both goals. I came back with a head as big as Birkenhead!

The following Saturday we played Chelsea at Burnden and I had a stinker; a real shocker. I could do nothing right. As we came off the field at the end, George was standing by the dressing room door. He always stood there and said 'Well done' to the lads or commiserated with us. 'Right, Lofty,' he says. 'I'll see you in my office on Monday morning.

Wembley, 1958. Bill Ridding and Jimmy Murphy, standing in for Matt Busby who was still recovering from his Munich injuries, lead the teams out.

Don't worry boss, we'll win! Bill Ridding looks anxious as he leads us out to face Manchester United — Bryan Edwards and John Higgins are behind me all the way.

Whoops! Harry Gregg misses a cross as I move in to challenge. Bill Foulkes looks on anxiously.

ONE UP. I beat grounded Harry Gregory and Stan Crowther to score the first after just three minutes.

Well, was it a goal? I bundle Gregg into the net for our second goal, one of Wembley's most controversial moments.

The moment every player dreams of . . . I receive the F.A. Cup from the Duke of Edinburgh.

Well played, Lofty! A victory hug from Bill Ridding.

Bolton Evening News

THE BUFF

TOUR MAY MAKE HISTORY FOR THE WANDERERS—Page 4

No. 28,186 SATURDAY, MAY 3, 1958 PRICE 2½d.

F.A. CUP COMES TO BOLTON

NAT starts his day of glory. This is his Goal No. 1

EDDIE HOPKINSON tips over the bar from Taylor.

RESULTS at a glance

F.A. CUP FINAL
(AT WEMBLEY)
Bolton W. 2 M'chester U. 0

GLASGOW CHARITY CUP
First Round
Celtic 1 Partick T. 0

Scottish League—Div. I
Clyde 2 Hibernian 1
Rangers 1 Airdrie 2

Scottish League—Div. II
Dundee Utd. 7 Berwick R. 0
Forfar Ath. 2 Dumbarton 0

R.L. Championship
(SEMI-FINALS)
St. Helens 13 W'kington 14

LOFTHOUSE SCORES TWICE AND PLAYS CAPTAIN'S PART IN THRILLING WEMBLEY FINAL

BOLTON WANDERERS 2, MANCHESTER UNITED 0

HOW THEY GOT THERE

WANDERERS		UNITED	
THIRD ROUND		THIRD ROUND	
A—PRESTON N.E. (Parry 2, Stevens)	3-0	A—WORKINGTON (Viollet 3)	3-1
FOURTH ROUND		FOURTH ROUND	
A—YORK CITY	0-0	H—IPSWICH TOWN (Charlton 2)	2-0
4th ROUND REPLAY		FIFTH ROUND	
H—YORK CITY (Allcock 2, Birch)	3-0	H—SHEFFIELD W. (Brennan 2, Dawson)	3-0
FIFTH ROUND		SIXTH ROUND	
H—STOKE CITY (Stevens, Lofthouse, Parry)	3-1	A—WEST BROMWICH A. (Taylor, Dawson)	2-2
SIXTH ROUND		6th ROUND REPLAY	
H—WOLVERHAMPTON (Stevens, Parry)	2-1	H—WEST BROMWICH A. (Webster)	1-0
SEMI-FINAL		SEMI-FINAL	
BLACKBURN R. (Gubbins 2) (At Maine-rd.)	2-1	FULHAM (Charlton 2) (At Villa Park)	2-2
		SEMI-FINAL REPLAY	
		FULHAM (Dawson 3, Charlton, Brennan) (At Highbury)	5-3

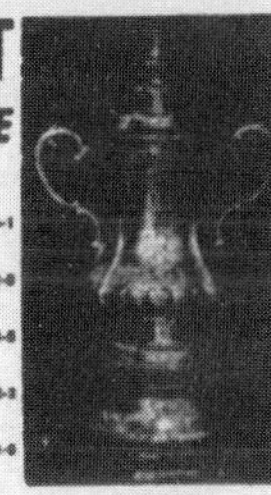

THE PRIZE

BOLTON WANDERERS
HOPKINSON
HARTLE BANKS
HENNIN HIGGINS EDWARDS (B.)
BIRCH STEVENS LOFTHOUSE PARRY HOLDEN
WEBSTER VIOLLET CHARLTON TAYLOR DAWSON
CROWTHER COPE GOODWIN
GREAVES FOULKES
GREGG
MANCHESTER UNITED
Referee: Mr. J. V. Sherlock (Sheffield).

LEMON-COLOURED BALL

VIOLLET MISSES

SEVERE TACKLES

CHEERS FOR HOPKINSON

BRILLIANT SAVES

A LET-OFF

Half-time: Bolton Wands. 1 Manchester U. 0

Sewell one up in golf final

Adlington Rangers win Evans Cup

New horse-shoe shaped course

CRICKET

GOLF CHAMPIONSHIP

Rugby League Championship semi-final

ST. HELENS BEATEN BY ONE POINT

SECOND-MINUTE GOAL

We've won . . . official! *The Bolton Evening News* Sports Special, Saturday May 3, 1958.

We've won the Cup! Brian Birch (left), Eddie Hopkinson and Derek Hennin join in the fun.

See the conquering heroes come . . . Bolton turns out in force as the Cup comes to town.

Speech! A vote of thanks for the fans . . . on my left, John Higgins and Roy Hartle seem to have heard it all before!

Bolton's 1958 Cup Final squad. Back row (left to right): Roy Hartle, John Higgins, Bryan Edwards, Eddie Hopkinson, Derek Hennin, Tommy Banks, Bert Sproston (trainer). Front: Brian Birch, Dennis Stevens, Nat Lofthouse, Bill Ridding, Ray Parry, Duggie Holden, Ralph Gubbins.

We'll meet again . . . Harry Gregg and I are still the best of pals 31 years after our Wembley dust-up.

8.30 sharp. 'Nay, George,' I said, 'Monday's our day off.' 'Not for you it isn't. In my office. 8.30.' Even then the message hadn't got through. I still thought he'd be wanting to congratulate me on my England debut. Tell me what a good game I'd had at Highbury.

Instead he gave me the biggest rollicking I've ever had — before or since. 'On Saturday afternoon, you were trying to do something you are just not capable of,' he told me when I arrived. 'And what's that, George?' 'Play football.' I thought . . . he's got to be winding me up here. 'You were coming back deep for the ball, trying to trap it. You couldn't trap a bag of wet cement. There are only three things you CAN do at this game. Run, shoot and head. That's what you did for England against Yugoslavia . . . why didn't you do it for us on Saturday? We've got plenty of people at this club who can turn on the fancy stuff. Leave that to them and concentrate on what you're good at.' It's the best piece of advice I ever received.

Yes, I was a bit clumsy . . . but put the ball between the centre-half and the full-back for me to run on to and I'd fancy my chances. Give me a decent cross to go for and it was never less than 50-50 between me and the centre-half.

George was a major influence on all the players, not just me. But of course, times were different then. We didn't really see ourselves as celebrities around the town. More part of the community.

Here's an example of my working day. I'd catch a bus down to the ground — it was a long time before I could afford a little car — arriving at 10 o'clock. Then training. I suppose today's players would look on it as a bit of a joke. We always trained out on the pitch. 10.15 start and half an hour's running round the track. Running, running, running. I must have been as fit as a fiddle. Then half an hour's ball work. No, not a football. One of those old heavy medicine balls, playing throw and catch and so on. Then body exercises. Finally they'd throw us a ball and say get on with some five-a-sides. But we were usually too knackered to do very much by then.

Nowadays, the ball is the big thing in training. that's what they play with on a Saturday afternoon so fair enough. It's the most important thing, isn't it?

But the game is still the same. When people ask me how I would get on nowadays when players are so much fitter I point to Finney, Matthews and Lawton. They would still be good players today. They would have the same skills. Perhaps with improved training techniques they would be even better players than we remember them. Now there's a thought.

After training we'd have a bite to eat and then home for the afternoon. A few odd jobs or a spot of gardening. Some of the lads got a little job in the afternoons to bring in a bit more. There were no sponsorship deals, no free cars, no personal appearances. When I signed on the groundstaff they paid me £3 a week. I used to clean out the dressing rooms, do the boots, that sort of thing. After the war I was on £10 a week in the summer and £12 a week in the season, with a £2 win bonus. The money went up over the years. £10 then £12, then £14 and in my last 12 months the princely sum of £17 a week.

But I didn't worry, I was proud to play for Bolton Wanderers. The club was proud of its reputation as a family club. Most of the 1958 Wembley side had been with the club for 12 years or more. That's one of two major reasons why team spirit was so high.

The other reason was the Burnden Park fans. I learned very early on that you won't find better fans anywhere. Yes, they've given some players a hard time over the years but by and large they're among the fairest in the game. They never criticise a trier.

I'll tell you how I picked up that lesson. In one of my early games, someone pushed a pass through between the centre-half and the left-back for me to run on to. Everyone on the ground could see he'd hit it too strong, that it was going out for a dead ball. But I thought I'd give it a go. I set off after that ball. I ran for 25 or 30 yards as if my life depended on it. And in the end I didn't miss it by much. It trickled over the line as I went sliding in. When I turned round to trot back to the centre circle for the goal kick I was given one of the biggest cheers I ever received. Just for trying. I remember thinking: 'Hey, Lofty, you've got something here. These people are cheering you just because you tried. You could have let that one go. You could have let the goalkeeper come out of his box, take the ball back in and then clear it upfield. But no, you gave it a try . . . and the fans love you for it.'

And they never changed. Oh yes, they'd give me some stick when I played badly. And I had my share of bad games, don't worry! But even then they'd tell me: 'You've had a bad 'un today, Lofty. But at least you tried.' A lot of Bolton players have shared those feelings down the years. It was a two-way thing. And I'm sure the loyalty of those fans played a big part in our two trips to Wembley in the fifties.

CHAPTER THREE

Wembley Wonderland

THE F.A. Cup. The very name has a magical ring for football people everywhere. I have never met a professional player who doesn't dream that one day he will play in the F.A. Cup Final at Wembley. The F.A. Cup is the most famous trophy in football. Wembley is the most famous stadium in the world. The Big One . . .

The F.A. Cup is the biggest domestic Soccer event in the world. The match is beamed live across the globe. People in hundreds of different countries watch it live. It is special. How many times have we had live coverage of the Spanish Cup Final from Barcelona or somewhere? Never! Have we ever had live television from the Dutch Cup Final? No. But there aren't many countries that don't take our Cup Final. There aren't many football people who don't recognise Wembley's twin towers instantly. There aren't many people who don't dream of winning the F.A. Cup.

I've been lucky enough to play in two F.A. Cup Finals . . . the Matthews Final in 1953 and the 1958 Final against the Manchester United side rebuilt from the ruins of the Munich tragedy.

They are days I will never forget. I've played for England at Wembley many times but it's a different feeling on Cup Final day. It has an atmosphere all of its own. When you stand in the tunnel at Wembley you might be in another world. All you can see of the stadium is a small square of light some 20 or 30 yards ahead. The other side lines up alongside you; there'll be a joke and a laugh but the tension is there. Then you start the long walk towards that square of light. When you reach the stadium, the sound hits you. One hundred thousand people cheer at once. The flags are waving, the scarves are waving. Trumpets blow. A wall of sound.

I never miss the Cup Final and when those two teams come marching out there's always a lump in my throat; the memories live again. I know just how those players feel. They wouldn't swop places with anyone else in the world.

All the great players have wanted to share this moment. People like Platini, Puskas and Pele have made a pilgrimage to Wembley to play in international matches or even representative matches or friendlies. Just to say they played there . . . But they never played in a Cup Final like those 22 men marching out there.

My only reservation about Cup Final day is that both teams should walk OFF the field together as well as ON to it together. It isn't a football match, it's a national event. Those players all play an equal part in the spectacle. Yet at the end of the match, one side takes the trophy, parades it round the pitch and celebrates . . . while the other side takes the long, lonely walk off the arena. By all means let the winners enjoy their hour of glory. Let them pause for the photographers. But when they start the lap of honour, the losers should be there alongside them. They have played their part, too. I should know. I've seen Wembley's big day from both sides. I know how it feels to win . . . and to lose.

Back at Bolton after the War, we always felt we were in with a chance in the F.A. Cup. Perhaps that stemmed from the very first peacetime competition when we went right through to the semi-final before losing to Charlton at Villa Park. That must have given us a taste for the battles ahead. But we had the ideal side for the F.A. Cup. We were always a good League side, finishing in the top ten in the First Division, but we were never really in with a serious shout for the Championship.

The Cup was different. No-one fancied their chances at Burnden Park and we weren't the kind of team to be rolled over by giantkillers. So, after a few near misses, we came to 1953.

We had the right blend. Billy Hughes, Bobby Langton and Duggie Holden, who was just coming through, were fast, skilful wingers. The inside forwards were Harold Hassall, with his strong, loping run and a fine shot, and Willie Moir, the skipper and brains of the side. I was in the middle. I could run, shoot and head. In the half-backs, Matt Barass was an out-and-out stopper, flanked by Johnny Wheeler, a fine attacking player, and Eric Bell. The full-backs were Johnny Ball and Ralph Banks, a good combination. Stan Hanson in goal didn't miss much.

A strong side with a good team spirit. The ideal Cup combination. We started along the road to Wembley with a home tie against Fulham, who had been relegated to Division Two the previous year. No real problems. We won 3-1.

It was a different story in the fourth round against another Second Division side, Notts County. They gave us a real battle. They held us 1-1 at home and took us back to Meadow Lane for a replay which also ended level at 2-2. We finally got them out of the way in the third match, winning 1-0 to earn ourselves a trip to another Second Division side, Luton Town. We beat them 1-0, too.

The quarter-final took us to Gateshead. Gateshead? Yes, they were still in the Football League in those days and the North East is not the sort of place anyone fancies going to with a Cup semi-final place at stake. But another 1-0 win took us into the last four.

Everton, who were having a spell in the Second Division, were waiting for us. And that Maine Road semi-final must go down as one of the most remarkable Cup battles of them all. We were 4-0 up at half-time. One step on that famous Wembley turf already. I had got two of them so I had more reason than most to be dreaming of those twin towers. But we ended up scraping through 4-3 as Everton hit us with everything but the kitchen sink. Perhaps we should have gone on the defensive but that wasn't our style. In fact it wasn't really anyone's style in those days. You rarely saw a team sitting on a lead.

But we took it a bit far that day. I remember thinking: 'What's going on here? We're throwing it away.' But it all turned out right in the end. People often say to me: 'Nat, you must have played well in the first half.' And I reply: 'Aye . . . but we must have been bad in the second!'

Before the celebrations even started we knew our Wembley opponents. Blackpool . . . and Stanley Matthews. Blackpool had been to Wembley twice before in the post-War years, losing to Manchester United in 1948 and Newcastle in 1950. Matthews was already a cult figure and everyone seemed to believe that 1953 would be his last chance to get a Cup winners medal. They thought his career was nearly over. It shows how wrong you can be.

But 1953 was a sentimental year. Queen Elizabeth the Second was crowned, Britain conquered Mount Everest, Sir Gordon Richards won his only Derby. Great things were happening to great people.

So you can understand why everybody — outside Bolton — wanted Blackpool to win the F.A. Cup. No-one, even in their wildest dreams, could have predicted how they would do it. Wembley, that famous old stadium, was preparing itself for one of the most thrilling football matches ever seen on that legendary turf.

CHAPTER FOUR

The Cup of Tears

EVERY club has its rituals before big games and at Bolton we were no exception along the road to that 1953 Wembley Final.

It involved The Cup Drink.

No, we didn't all go out on the town the night before every round . . . but we had to partake of the great drink. It meant mixing two dozen eggs in a couple of bottles of sherry. Stir it all up and gulp it down. Shared among all the members of the team, that is. Before every round of the Cup we'd drink this potion after training because it would build us up, do us good. If it was such good stuff, why didn't we have it every week? We'd have been world beaters! Anyway, The Cup Drink did the trick for us that year all right, so there must have been something in it.

It may sound odd these days but we made no special preparations for the Blackpool match. No, I'm not going to say 'it was just another game.' It wasn't, it was the F.A. Cup Final. But it was very much business as usual in the weeks between our semi-final win over Everton and Wembley. We had a couple of days at the seaside — Blackpool of all places — getting the clean sea air into our lungs as they say. And, of course, we had to get fitted out for the big day. Jackson's the Tailors I think it was who provided the suits, shirts and ties. We might not have been the best team in the world but we were certainly the smartest. Or we thought so, anyway!

Of course the people of Bolton had no intention of letting this one pass as just another game. While it wasn't exactly a local derby, Blackpool was only about 30 miles down the road and the place where Bolton folk went for their summer holidays. So there was no shortage of Red Rose rivalry. I lost count of the number of times I was hailed in the streets with: 'Don't bother coming home if you don't bring the Cup with you, Lofty!' Tickets were like gold dust. Over 50,000 people used to stand on the terraces at Burnden Park and they all wanted a ticket for this one. I never knew I had so many friends.

But fair enough. The Cup Final is the biggest day in the English Soccer calendar and if your home town team is playing in it you want to be there. We left for our big-match headquarters in Reading on the Thursday and if any of us had tried to pretend this was just another game, we knew by now that it wasn't. Our wives and families were due to travel down on the Saturday morning and join us after the match for, we hoped, the celebration party.

And for me there was an extra honour. I was voted Footballer of the Year by the Football Writers Association. It had been a good season for me. I'd scored 22 goals in 36 games and played eight times for England, scoring eight goals. I was proud to collect that famous award at the traditional eve of Wembley dinner. But it wasn't just for me. It was for my team-mates who made it possible and the Bolton fans who had supported us through thick and thin.

Now we wanted to give them the icing on the cake . . . the F.A. Cup. It was a beautiful day as we marched out into that sea of scarves, rosettes and banners. Orange and white at the end; navy blue and white at the other. And a royal occasion, too. In her Coronation Year, the Queen was here at Wembley to present the Cup. All over the country, people had bought their first television set to watch her Coronation. Now, with less than a month to go before that great day, they tuned into another time-honoured British tradition, the F.A. Cup Final. For many people who had never been to Wembley, it was their first glimpse of live action from the Empire Stadium.

Here's how the two sides lined up:

BOLTON: Hanson, Ball, R. Banks, Wheeler, Barass, Bell, Holden, Moir, Lofthouse, Hassall, Langton.

BLACKPOOL: Farm, Shimwell, Garrett, Fenton, Johnston, Robinson, Matthews, Taylor, Mortenson, Mudie, Perry.

We knew only too well that everyone outside Bolton wanted Blackpool to win and Stanley Matthews to collect that elusive medal. But I don't think that feeling affected our preparation for the match. We didn't let it worry us. If I hadn't been playing for Bolton Wanderers I would have wanted Stanley to get his winners medal just like everybody else. The important difference was that I DID play for Bolton and I wanted that medal, too.

And for 66 minutes of a great Wembley occasion I had no reason to believe I wasn't going to get it. Only two minutes had gone when I scored to put us in front. It won't go down as one of my greatest goals — but they all count. Duggie Holden's pass put me in the clear with only George Farm, the Blackpool keeper, to beat. I didn't hit the shot properly and it must have bounced three times before it got to Farm. But George made a complete mess of it. Whether he dived too early or took his eye off the ball I don't know. But it hit him on the shoulder and bounced into the net.

What a start! They say every Cup Final needs an early goal and we certainly provided one that day. It settled us down perfectly. Little did we know what fate — and Blackpool — had in store for us. After just 18 minutes our left-half Eric Bell went down with a hamstring injury. He was crippled. He struggled on but we had to reorganise completely. There were no substitutes then. Eric went on to the left wing. That's where we always put a passenger in those days. That meant Bobby Langton switching to inside-left and Harold Hassall moved back to take Eric's place at left-half.

Fifteen minutes after the blow of Eric's injury, Blackpool were level when Stan Mortenson scored with a low shot that touched Hasall on its way past Stan Hanson. But after 38 minutes Willie Moir moved in to put us 2-1 up and we were happy the way things had gone as we left the field at half-time. As we walked towards the Wembley tunnel a voice called out: 'Congratulations, Lofty!' It was Morty. 'What for?' I asked him, 'We haven't won yet, you know.' 'I know you haven't' he replied. 'But don't you realise you've scored in every round?'

A great gesture from a great player, a sporting opponent and a fine man. And Morty's part in that Cup Final was far from over. We seemed on the way to victory when Bell, despite his injury, got up to head past Farm and put us 3-1 up after 55 minutes. We had one hand on the trophy.

Three men thought otherwise. Morty, Ernie Taylor and Matthews. You'll probably find it hard to believe but we had made no special plans to deal with the threat from Matthews. Yes, he was a great player and a matchwinner but we were happy with our own ability to deal with him. And for 66 minutes you couldn't argue with that thinking. We were 3-1 up in the Cup Final despite having one of our key men, Eric Bell, a passenger on the left wing.

But we had, crucially, been forced into a reshuffle that took Harold Hassall out of the front line and forced Bobby Langton, one of the game's best wingers, inside. Outside him he had a limping Eric Bell. In that fateful 66th minute, Taylor fed Matthews with just the kind of ball he liked . . . to his feet. Stanley always used to tell players: 'I want the ball at my feet. I'm not going to run for it. When I get the ball I need all my energy to do what I'm here for . . . beat people. I'm not going to waste energy running for it.' This time Matthews took on the defence, crossed and there was Morty to head into the net. 3-2.

We clung on. But the tide had turned. We knew it. Blackpool knew it. And with just two minutes to go they were level. They were awarded a free-kick on the edge of the box and up stepped Morty to smack it into the back of the net. His hat-trick. The first player to score three in a Wembley Cup Final. And the team everyone had given up for dead had risen from the ashes.

We couldn't believe what had happened. How can you control a match for so long and see it suddenly go wrong? I know I had gone a bit. We all had. The rest was inevitable. We held out until 20 seconds from the end until Matthews got away again, sent over one of those inch-perfect crosses . . . and there was Bill Perry to score the winner.

So the incredible Matthews Final was over. It was Blackpool's Harry Johnston not our own Willie Moir who hoisted the famous trophy aloft. Stanley, the oldest man on the field at 38, had his medal and we had our might-have-beens.

But while that 1953 Final will always go down as Stanley's game, let's not forget two men who made it possible for Matthews to join Harry on his team-mates' shoulders as they paraded the Cup.

First, Stanley Mortenson. No-one who scores a hat-trick in a Cup Final should ever be forgotten, and remember Morty got his goals for a side that looked to be on the way to defeat. Like me he scored in every round that year.

And then there's little Ernie Taylor, the true unsung hero of Wembley, 1953. It wasn't until Ernie started hitting those slide-rule passes to Stanley's feet that the great man began to put his indelible stamp on the match. Once he did, our fate was sealed.

You can never have regrets about playing in a Cup Final, even when you lose. Just to be there is the one thing no-one can ever take away from you. We shared a drink with the Blackpool players that night. I was glad for Morty, Ernie, Harry Johnston and Stanley. We were England players together. We'd all taken part in a thrilling Final. Maybe not the greatest football match Wembley has ever seen but probably the most thrilling spectacle. And, above all, the Cup Final is a spectacle.

But as I walked off the Wembley pitch after collecting my loser's medal I vowed to myself: 'I'll be back.' I was. But I had to wait five years. And once again Bolton Wanderers and Nat Lofthouse were destined to play their part in one of Wembley's most emotional occasions.

CHAPTER FIVE

The Cup That Cheers

AS the Blackpool players and their supporters celebrated their Wembley triumph and we were left with our dreams of what might have been, another Soccer dream was taking shape ten miles down the road from Burnden Park. It was the dream of Matt Busby, arguably the greatest manager of them all. Even as the Manchester United side of the late forties and early fifties was carrying all before it, Matt conceived the idea of building a team all of his own: a team that graduated through the juniors at Old Trafford. The Busby Babes.

Games between Manchester United and Bolton were always an occasion. We had some tremendous battles against men like Johnny Carey, Johnny Morris, Jack Rowley, Henry Cockburn and the rest. There was always a special feeling before those games. There was that extra bit of tension in the air. You felt that one slip could decide the match . . . and you didn't want to be the man who made that slip. And when the team that won the F.A. Cup in 1948 and the League title four years later began to fade, the Babes came along. They were different, special. They were all young, exuberant and so skilful. I was lucky enough to play alongside three of them in the England side: Tommy Taylor, Roger Byrne and Duncan Edwards.

I first met Tommy Taylor on England's 1954 tour of South America. We spent eight weeks together and I have no hesitation in saying that if he hadn't died in the Munich air crash he would have become the greatest centre-forward of them all. Matt Busby had taken him to Old Trafford from Barnsley as a raw teenager, paying — and this is typical of Matt — £29,999 9s 11d. He didn't want Tommy to shoulder the burden of being the first £30,000 player. It soon became obvious that he was an exceptional player. Tommy Lawton was brilliant in the air, good on the ground. I was good upstairs and not so good downstairs. Morty could run and shoot but he had a few weaknesses. So had Jackie Milburn. I don't recall Tommy Taylor having any weaknesses at all.

Roger Byrne was the captain of the Busby Babes. He seemed like a father figure yet he was only a young man himself. He was a classic player, a great football brain. He was experienced beyond his years on and off the field. There is no doubt that if he had survived Munich he would have gone on to become one of England's great captains. And then there was Duncan Edwards. Big Dunc. What a man. What a player. So full of life, so full of fun. He would play anywhere, any time. He would have turned out for United or England without boots on. He would have played at outside left or right back. Anywhere just to get a game. At 18, he was already a grown man. A footballer at the height of his powers.

Duncan scored the finest goal I have ever seen. West Germany v England in the Olympic Stadium, Berlin, 1956. England won 3-1. Duncan called for a throw out from our keeper Reg Matthews on the left-hand side of the penalty box. He beat one man, advanced to the halfway line, beat another, beat three more inside the German half and from 30 yards hit a left-footer that went into the net like a rocket.

There was some party that night. England had won 3-1 against the 1954 World Cup winners and Duncan Edwards had scored that goal. Duncan led the celebrations. He was that kind of man. He lived life to the full.

But for the Munich air crash, England would have had the finest side in their history. No doubt about it. Roger, Tommy and Big Duncan were already in the team. Eddie Colman, David Pegg and Mark Jones would have joined them. Dennis Violett and, of course, Bobby Charlton survived Munich and went on to play for England.

We used to have some tremendous games against them. I recall one night in the fog at Burnden Park — I wasn't playing — when we beat them 6-3. We played them at Old Trafford on the night they switched on the floodlights and spoiled the party by winning 2-0.

But it wasn't all one-way traffic. Far from it. In late January, 1958, they beat us 7-2 at Old Trafford. Beat us? No, they annihilated us. I scored our second goal with a few minutes left, challenging Harry Gregg for a high cross — does that sound familiar? Anyway the ball went in the net and the referee gave a goal. He must have felt sorry for us. I suppose 7-2 sounds better than 7-1.

Anyway, I was sitting in the United dressing room with them afterwards. We always used to drink bottles of Double Diamond. No glasses, straight out of the bottle. They were all there . . . Big Dunc, Tommy, Mark Jones, David Pegg, Eddie Colman, Roger. 'We had you going in the last ten minutes,' I joked. 'I could tell you were worried!'

Sixteen days later, they were dead.

The word 'great' is used too lightly these days. You only have to turn on the television to see a 'great' pass, pick up a paper to read about a 'great' game, switch on the radio to hear about a 'great' goal. They can't all be great. But the Busby Babes were. Great players, a great team, great people. Great days. Their death stunned the world. Not just Manchester, not just Lancashire, not just Britain. The world.

I was running a pub in Bolton at the time, the Castle Hotel. I heard on the six o'clock news that the Manchester United plane had crashed in Munich on the way home from their European Cup quarter-final against Red Star Belgrade. I couldn't believe it. No-one could.

Like everyone else in football, my sympathies were with United all the way. Jimmy Murphy, who took charge while Matt Busby was recovering in hospital, didn't just have the usual problems of picking a team. He had to FIND a team. Harry Gregg, Bill Foulkes and Bobby Charlton came back from Munich. He signed men like Ernie Taylor and Stan Crowther. Ian Greaves, Alex Dawson, Mark Pearson and others came into the side and worked miracles. Their fight stirred the emotions of the whole nation. Their battle against adversity to the gates of Wembley was an epic journey.

And waiting for them in that 1958 Cup Final were Bolton Wanderers. Just as in 1953, we were the team no-one outside Bolton wanted to win. But, just as in 1953, we were there to win the Cup. This time we didn't intend to fail.

The Bolton side that had gone so close in the Matthews Final had broken up. We started the 1958 Cup campaign with a tried and trusted combination that included just two of the men who played against Blackpool, Doug Holden and myself. I was now the skipper. And while the 1953 side was probably more skilful, this was a tremendous team in the true sense of the word. We had all been signed on for the basic £10 fee. They called us the £110 team. They used to say that if you kicked one man in the side you had to kick 'em all.

In goal we had Eddie Hopkinson, who went on to play 14 times for England. The full-backs were that legendary pairing of Roy Hartle and Tommy Banks — Mr Hartle and Mr Banks to you.

They had a reputation of being hard men. Let's put it this way . . . I used to wear my shin pads at the back of my legs and I was on their side. Hard. Yes. But fair. Good men. Good players.

John Higgins at centre-half was a big man, a stopper pure and simple. And he stopped 'em.

Derek Henning at right-half would run all day and at left-half we had Bryan Edwards. He never had a bad game. Before every match he would put two rolls of elastoplast on each ankle just to get him on to the pitch. We used to cal him Nijinsky. But he never gave up. He was always there when you needed him.

Duggie Holden was still a great winger on the left flank and on the other side we had Brian Birch, very similar in style. Ray Parry at inside-left kept pounding in those tremendous shots and in Dennis Stevens we had one of the most underrated players of them all.

He was a real tiger, a typical old-fashioned inside forward. He never stopped, always looking for the ball out of defence and starting an attack. And there I was, still in the middle, still running, shooting and heading — just like George Taylor had told me after that first game for England back in 1950.

Most of those players spent their whole career at Bolton. Of course clubs wanted to sign them. But they were happy to stay. It was that kind of set-up. No stars. A great team.

We needed to be when we heard the draw for the third round. Preston North End away! Finney still at the height of his powers, Docherty still a regular for Scotland. And many more.

Like us Preston had sampled the sour taste of defeat at Wembley when they lost to West Brom in 1954. Finney wanted to go back, too.

But two goals from Ray Parry and another from Dennis Stevens gave us a wonderful send-off along the long road to Wembley.

The fourth round served up another tough one . . . York City away. York may have been in the Third Division but three years earlier they had gone further than any other Third Division side when they forced Newcastle to a semi-final replay before going out.

We knew this one would be hard all right. We drew 0-0 at Bootham Crescent and I was ruled out of the replay through injury. But we got through 2-0 and prepared for another hard game in the fifth round. Stoke City. I got the first goal in our 3-1 win, Dennis Stevens and Ray Parry scoring the others. But victory only threw up yet another hard tie, in fact the hardest of them all. Wolves at Burnden Park. We knew by then that if we were going to Wembley in 1958, it was going to be the hard way.

Under Stan Cullis Wolves were, with the Busby Babes, the outstanding team of the fifties. They won the Championship in 1953, 1958 and 1959 and the Cup in 1960. The side was packed with internationals throughout the decade. Billy Wright was an automatic choice as England skipper and men like Bill Slater, Bert Williams, Ron Flowers, Jesse Pye, Jimmy Mullen, Johnny Hancocks and Peter Broadbent won more than their fair share of caps.

A formidable team. But in a memorable game before a packed Burnden, we beat them 2-1 to go into the last four. Derek Hennin was injured early on and had to hobble off and Ray Parry was concussed soon after scoring our second goal. But we hung on in the face of a relentless barrage in the closing minutes.

In the semi-final we were off to Maine Road again, scene of our thriller against Everton five years earlier. Once again the opposition was from Lancashire — Blackburn Rovers. They were a fair side and went to Wembley themselves two years later. With men like Ronnie Clayton, Brian Douglas and Peter Dobing around it was never going to be easy. And it was even tougher for me because I had to sit on the sidelines. I broke my shoulder four weeks earlier at Tottenham, so I was on the bench with my arm in a sling as my team-mates battled their way to Wembley. Ralph Gubbins took my place at centre-forward and scored both the goals in our 2-0 win. What's more, I wouldn't have scored either of them. Both came from inside the penalty box and for both he needed close control and good footwork. Never my strong points.

We didn't learn for four days who we'd be playing. United drew 2-2 with Fulham at Villa Park. It seemed the football world held its breath as they waited for the midweek replay at Highbury. No mistake this time. United were through, winning 4-3. The dream had come true.

The 1958 Cup Final will not be remembered as a great Final. It will be remembered for the emotion. The team that died at Munich had risen from the ashes. The nation waited for the fairy story to have a happy ending.

This was the Wembley line-up:

BOLTON: Hopkinson, Hartle, T. Banks, Hennin, Higgins, Edwards, Birch, Stevens, Lofthouse, Parry, Holden.

MANCHESTER UNITED: Gregg, Foulkes, Greaves, Goodwin, Cope, Crowther, Dawson, Taylor, Charlton, Viollet, Webster.

Within a few minutes of the start, we were one up. Two Cup Finals, two early goals. This time Bryan Edwards picked up a loose United clearance and, as their defence came out, slipped through a diagonal pass for me to run on to. Perfect.

You never really remember the exact feeling when you've scored a goal. I just recall racing back to the halfway line and getting ready to start again. We were one up in the Cup Final.

And this time there were no mistakes. We were the better team throughout. As I've said, United worked a miracle even to get a team together, let alone reach the Cup Final. We were a strong, experienced First Division side. This was a match we knew we should win. It would have been very different if we'd been playing the Busby Babes. We MIGHT have won that one. We might not! But what a Final that would have been! But against this patched-up team we were always going to be in the driving seat. We simply dare not let sentiment and our personal feelings about Munich creep into it. We had a job to do. For ourselves. For our fans.

The only moment's doubt I had was when Bobby Charlton unleashed one of his 25-yarders that rebounded off the post with Hopkinson beaten. If that had gone in, things might have been different. That little word 'if' . . . but it didn't. Instead, my second goal decided the match — and sparked a Soccer row that still lives today whenever that game is discussed.

Here's how it happened. Dennis Stevens fired in a shot from the left-hand side of the box that Harry Gregg stopped but couldn't hold. Perhaps he was surprised by the pace of the ball. I don't know. But I was following in at top speed. I saw Gregg turn to catch the ball and then I hit him, the ball, the lot into the back of the net. A foul? Looking back, yes. Today I would probably have been sent off. But in those days you could challenge the keeper. That's what I did. I didn't go in to hurt Gregg. I went for the ball. And that's how the referee saw it. When I looked round he was pointing to the centre circle. Goal. I don't argue with referees!

I'll tell you what, though. I'm glad we won that match 2-0. I wouldn't have wanted our moment of triumph to be soured by a controversial goal. People often ask me if Harry and I speak to one another these days. Of course. We were speaking to one another after that Cup Final, sharing a drink. He was a guest at my testimonial dinner. I see Harry three or four times a year and the one thing we never talk about in any detail is the 1958 Cup Final. That's in the past. We talk about today's game, today's players, the future. If he has to stand up and make a speech . . . that's a different story. I get the whole lot, chapter and verse. But there's no ill feeling.

And what a different feeling there was when the final whistle blew on that historic May day. We had won. This time WE went up for the Cup. And I honestly can't recall my emotions as I received the trophy from Prince Philip and held it aloft. I just recall holding that precious piece of silver and handing it to the rest of the lads in turn so that they could do the same. Do you remember Nobby Stiles after England had won the World Cup in 1966? Remember how he put the trophy on his head and danced with delight? A little Punch and Judy Show. That's how it feels to win at Wembley. That's how we felt after beating Manchester United. You can imagine the party in our dressing room afterwards. The Cup was on the table, the drink was flowing. What a day.

Then there came a knock on the door. In walked Matt Busby.

Matt was still struggling to recover from the injuries he received at Munich. He walked with a stick. Jimmy Murphy walked alongside, lending him a hand. In complete silence, Matt walked round our dressing room, shaking every player by the hand. He congratulated us all individually. Something — something very special — made that man come into our dressing room in what must have been one of the saddest moments of his life to congratulate us on beating his team. Tommy Banks summed it up for us all when he said, after Matt had hobbled quietly away: 'That's the finest sportsman you'll ever see.' No wonder Matt's teams always played for him. How could you fail to respect a man like that?

CHAPTER SIX

England My England

I'M a lucky lad. Thanks to football I've seen the world, met some wonderful people and shared some marvellous times as an England player.

Pulling on that white shirt always meant a lot to me. I was always proud. Like the Cup Final, it's something every player dreams of but few achieve. It's a special sort of feeling going out there to play for your country. Walking out at Wembley knowing you're playing for England, that the fans out there are all wanting you to win. Or, away from home, all wanting you to lose!

The first hint that I might be on the road to an England cap came in 1949 when I was named for an F.A. XI against the RAF at Stoke. We lost 7-5 but I scored four times, three of them from crosses by Stanley Matthews, and I had savoured the taste of representative football.

The next step on the ladder in those days was the Football League side. It was like a trial run for the England team. They would name some regular internationals as well as a few up and coming youngsters. I played my first game against the Irish League at Wolverhampton in February, 1950.

Over the years I played 13 representative games for the League, picking up 21 goals, including a record haul of six against the Irish League at Wolverhampton in 1952.

My big break came in the summer of 1950 when I was chosen for the F.A. tour of Canada. The main England team was involved in the World Cup in Uruguay but we still had some fine players on that tour. Men like Jimmy Hagan, Tim Ward, my Bolton colleague Stan Hanson, Johnny Hancocks, Jackie Sewell . . . and a chap called Stanley Matthews, who for some reason, was not in the World Cup squad.

It was a great trip, particularly for someone like me who had never been abroad . . . I used to say I took a foreign holiday when I went to the Isle of Man! We sailed on the *Empress of Canada*, did our training on board ship and over the next eight weeks played 14 matches in places like Quebec, Toronto, Saskatchewan and Vancouver.

One of the highlights for me was the day I played AGAINST England! When we arrived in Saskatchewan, the local team were two men short, so Tim Ward and I volunteered to play for them. I kicked off 20 times that day . . . we lost 19-1. What's more, I didn't get the one!

We also crossed into North America for a game against a Yankee XI in New York. We won 6-3 . . . which is more than could be said for the England team in the World Cup. They lost to the Americans 1-0 at Belo Horizonte. That was a helluva shock. Nothing like it had ever happened before.

I came back with my sights firmly set on an England place. But there was some pretty stiff opposition lined up against me. For two years after the end of the War, my idol Tommy Lawton had held the job. One of the all-time greats.

When he dropped out, men like Jackie Milburn, Stan Mortenson, Jesse Pye, Jack Rowley and Roy Bentley stepped into the frame. And, in 1950, Nat Lofthouse.

In those days a centre-forward was expected to score goals. Remember that advice Tommy Lawton gave me? 'Nat, always try to score.' Well that was the way. If you weren't scoring goals, you weren't in the side. Club or country. Now Stan Mortenson always scored goals, 23 in 25 games for England. He was one of the bravest players I have ever seen. I've known Morty put his head where you wouldn't put an iron bar. He would go for anything, in the air or on the ground. His only weakness was his lack of height. A few more inches and he really would have been some player.

I always felt Jackie Milburn's best position was on the wing. He could catch pigeons. You won't see many faster players than Jackie. But somehow, he never quite seemed to have the heart to be a centre-forward.

If you're playing number nine you've got to go for everything in the box. You're going to get hit, you're going to get hurt. Out on the wing, there's more chance to take a player on one to one. That was Jackie's strength. He had a great shot in either foot yet funnily enough the goal I remember most was his header for Newcastle in the 1955 Cup Final against Manchester City. He didn't get many with his head, Jackie, but he got one when it mattered that day.

Roy Bentley scored some great goals for Chelsea. He was a fine player on the deck but he was the kind of player who needs someone alongside him to take the knocks. He wasn't a robust man. I used to relish the 50-50 challenge, in the air or on the ground, with a big centre-half. That was always part of my game. Not Roy. But he still scored a lot of good goals. A good guy.

And, like I say, there were men like Jesse Pye of Wolves and Jack Rowley of Manchester United in contention. That was before the greatest of them all came along, Tommy Taylor.

I was sitting at home in Temple Road with my wife Alma when I heard on the radio that I was in the England team to play Yugoslavia at Highbury in November, 1950. We'd been married three years and my son Jeff had just been born.

I'd taken out a £900 mortgage with repayments of £6 a month. 'You've put a rope round your neck for life,' said my Dad. He earned £2 10 shillings a week as a coalbagger and here was I about to get £30 for 90 minutes' football . . . complete with the honour of an England cap.

I don't mind admitting it made me think. Take off the tax and that one game would pay off the mortgage for three months. I never had a lot of brain but it didn't take me long to work out that if I stayed in the England team I'd be all right.

I eventually received an official letter asking me to report to the Great Western Hotel in Paddington and after that we transferred to our match headquarters in Weybridge. The first person to congratulate me was Morty, one of the men in line for that number nine shirt. Like I say, a great guy.

But even though I scored both our goals in the 2-2 draw, I had to wait another 11 months and four matches before I was picked again. But I had no cause for complaint. As my coach at Bolton, George Taylor, had told me with some force, it wasn't just me out there at Highbury; there were 10 other players who had all played their part.

So when I wasn't in the side to play Scotland at Wembley in April, 1951, I didn't beef about it. I didn't grumble because I hadn't got a letter or a telephone call from the manager explaining why I was dropped.

Why should I? I'll tell you why I was dropped . . . because they had someone better to put in. Stan Mortenson. The important thing was that I had played for England. I'd been blooded. They knew about me. I'd gone to London, pulled on that white shirt and scored two goals. That was a gift to me, not a right. Now, if someone was playing better than me he deserved to be in the side ahead of me. It was up to me to prove I was worth another chance. When I did get that chance, against

Wales in the autumn of 1951, I took it. I played in the next 18 games, scoring 18 goals.

Walter Winterbottom was the manager for every one of my 33 England appearances. He was a great guy. All the players had a tremendous amount of respect for Walter. I don't think anyone in the world could have got more out of his players. He knew exactly what man management was all about.

Respect isn't something you buy. It's something you earn, something you work for. When we were abroad we would go out for a drink in the evening. Walter would ask us to be back for 10.30. We would be back for 10.25. If any of the lads started talking about staying out a bit longer they would soon be put straight. 'Walter wants us in for 10.30. We'll be in for 10.30,' he would be told.

We would often go to official functions in big hotels. If any of the lads started to get a bit noisy it only needed one look from Walter to calm us down. He would say to us: 'Enjoy yourselves, lads. But don't disgrace yourselves.' That's all it needed.

He would study the opposition in great detail and before every game would talk to each player about the man who would be marking him. Here's a typical example.

'Nat,' he would say in that educated voice. 'This chap is 13 stone and 6ft 1in. He's strong on the right foot, weak on the left. And he's not too good upstairs.' Then he'd turn to Finney and Matthews. 'So Tom, Stanley, can you get those balls over in the air for Nat, please? Good show!

'Oh, and Nat . . . don't go near the keeper. It will only cause trouble and we've enough problems here as it is.' I knew exactly where I stood. He wasn't telling me what to do. He knew what I could do because that was why I'd been picked. He told me about my opponent. It was the same with the rest of the team.

So I knew what was involved. I knew my man was no good upstairs. 'Right, get 'em over, Stan. Get 'em over, Tom,' I'd say. 'I'm one up on this guy already.'

Walter always wore the same expression no matter how we were playing. If we were doing badly he would walk quietly round at half-time saying: 'We can do better than this. You can all play better.' There was no ranting and raving. And if we had played well and won, he didn't go crazy about it either. You knew exactly where you stood with him.

Looking back at my time with Walter I can understand how today's England players are feeling. The Press keep hounding Bobby Robson, the manager, but the players have stood by him. I admire them for that.

They're the men who are living, eating and drinking with Robson. They're the men who have to go out there and do it for him on the pitch. And it's obvious to me that they respect him. The players know more about the manager than any Press man. His life is in their hands.

I had the same amount of respect for Billy Wright who was captain of England in just about every game I played. Billy was a great player but above all he was a great captain, a true leader. He might be having a stinker but that didn't stop him shouting and encouraging all the other players around him. He never let his own performance affect his captaincy. Mind you, I always fancied my chances when I played against Billy. I could outrun and outjump him. So I looked forward to our meetings. Which couldn't be said of all the centre-halves I came up against. There were three in particular who always gave me a hard time: Stan Cullis of Wolves, Neil Franklin of Stoke and Manchester City's Dave Ewing.

I could always understand my problems with Franklin and Cullis. They were clever players, read the game well. They seemed to be one step ahead of me all the time.

Dave was different. He was a big man, a pure stopper. And when you ran into Big Dave you stopped! Every time we played City I'd say: 'I've got to beat this devil today.' But I never did. I'd play like a real donkey. Dave always came out on top.

With Billy Wright I was always confident. But that doesn't mean he always had a bad game against me. Far from it. For Wolves and England he had the knack of getting the team to fit in around him. If he was struggling, someone else would cover up. He was a wholehearted player and a great skipper. He deserved every one of his 105 caps.

Another man who got the acclaim he deserved was Alf Ramsey. I played a lot with Alf and he always had his own game in order. He knew exactly what he was doing. He was captain in my first international. Billy Wright was injured. And I remember he went out of his way to make me feel at home. I was the only new cap in the side.

And I've never known such a cool customer on the field. Here's what I mean. Austria gave us a hard time in a match at Wembley in 1952. They led 1-0 and it could have been three or four when we were awarded a penalty. Alf always took the penalties.

Now he had worked out this theory that the best way to keep the ball low from the penalty spot was to have the lace facing the keeper. Only this time the ball refused to stay on the spot whenever Alf pointed the lace towards goal.

It seemed to take an age before he got that ball how he wanted it. The fans must have wondered what was going on. But Alf was totally unruffled and calmly stroked the ball past Zemen for the equaliser.

Alf didn't just have his own game in order. He could put everyone else right, too. He didn't just think: 'I'm having a good 'un, never mind the rest.' He would help us all. He was such a brainy player. If things weren't going so well he would take me aside at half-time and say try this, try that. 'Delay your run a bit and I'll be able to put the ball where you want it.'

He did, too. He could always spot where players were going wrong so it was no surprise to me when he became such a successful manager. Alf was probably the best reader of the game I ever played with. When he became England manager and announced that we would win the World Cup in 1966 I didn't doubt him for a minute. I knew him. Alf didn't THINK we might win; he didn't HOPE we would win it. He KNEW we would and said so. He was right.

Like I say, I was a lucky lad to play for England. I was even luckier that so often I had Tom Finney and Stanley Matthews in the same team. Some of the continental players we came up against were good. But they couldn't touch Tom and Stanley. With those two in the side anyone could play centre-forward.

If one of them played in the same team as me it was brilliant. If they both played it was out of this world. Two reasons why I scored a lot of goals for England? Matthews and Finney. I played 22 games for England when Tom Finney was on the left-wing. I scored 22 goals. Coincidence? No way. As soon as I knew I was in the side I looked to see if Tom's name was there, too.

I remember once reading in an England match report that 'Nat Lofthouse started another England attack by passing to Tom Finney.' Every time I got the ball I passed it to Tom Finney!

In fact there were many times when I looked for Tom and he wasn't even playing! I relied on him. He knew my strengths, my weaknesses. He knew where I liked the ball. He knew I could run, shoot and head and not much more. I knew he would put the ball exactly where I wanted it.

Tom was the complete team man. He could play in any forward position. He played in four different positions for England. In those days the side was chosen by a selection committee. Alf Ramsey was the first manager with complete control of team selection. And I sometimes used to think the committee saved Tom for a position where they had a weakness. You see, Tom had no weaknesses at all.

He was a great player on the field and a great man off it. He would help anyone. I remember once going to a testimonial match in Grimsby with him. He picked me up at Burnden Park at noon and we didn't get back until three o'clock the next morning. But that didn't worry Tom. He was just pleased he could use his name to help another player. He's been like that all his life. Tom only lived 20 miles or so down the road in Preston. Our wives were good friends and we saw a lot of one another on and off the field. I owe him a lot.

It's hard to believe that Tom wasn't an automatic choice for England. But there were a lot of good wingers around. Men like our own Bobby Langton, Jimmy Mullen and Johnny Hancocks of Wolves, Les Medley of Spurs, Jackie Milburn . . . and Stanley Matthews.

There was only one Stan Matthews. We'll never see anyone like him again. Unique. I freely admit that if I'd had a gun at the end of the 1953 Final I would have shot him! But think of all the memories I would have missed by not having him in the England side.

Stanley knew exactly what he wanted. He had his own ideals. He didn't train with the rest of the side because he knew how he must train to suit his own game. You would see him out there doing short sprints, one after the other, He was careful what he ate. He never drank or smoked. He looked after his health. He was precise in everything. Things had to be just right. They threw the pattern away when they made him. I've seen him come off the field in a Wembley international because his boots didn't feel quite right. He would tell me before the match: 'Don't come out on to my wing, Nat. You'll only bring a defender with you. Leave me to get to the by-line and then I'll get the ball over . . . lace away so it won't hurt when you head it!' He always tried to build you up.

Stanley didn't like three things. Swearing, smoking . . . and the ball three yards either side of him! He wanted the ball at his feet every time. And funnily enough I don't recall ever seeing him head a ball.

He didn't score many goals, in fact, I honestly think Stanley got more pleasure seeing someone score from one of his passes than he did actually scoring himself . He wasn't as easy to play with as Tom . . . but I'm not complaining. Tom knew exactly where I wanted the ball; Stanley knew exactly where he was going to put it. It was up to me to be there when it arrived.

It was uncanny. Stanley's crosses were never to the near post, never to the far post. Always on the penalty spot . . . or just a few yards in towards the goal. Just enough to have the keeper in two minds.

I had to judge how far Stan had to run to get to the by-line, to anticipate when he would cross the ball. Then I started my run. The secret was to come thundering in just as that ball floated over the penalty spot. Nine times out of ten it would come.

Stanley was very easy to get on with. On that first F.A. tour to Canada I spent eight weeks with him and never had any problems. He was great. When we landed in Canada all the Press rushed up the gangway to get a picture of Stanley Matthews, the world's number one footballer. 'Smile please, Mr Matthews,' they cried. We were left standing around. But Stanley saw what was happening. 'Just a moment, gentlemen,' he said. 'We have come here as a team and we shall have a team picture. Come on lads.' That sums up the man. Throughout the trip he would be asked to make an appearance at a shop or something like that and he would always insist that two or three of the lads were invited too.

Yes, he had his own lifestyle. Played the game his way. But he was the best. And a great guy, too. Fantastic. But playing for England in those days you were always part of a team. I've talked of some of the stars but we all depended on one another. Stanley needed the other ten because we were there to give him the ball.

And there were plenty of other fine players. Like Jimmy Dickinson. He played over 800 games for Portsmouth. That speaks for itself. Never had a bad game. I've always placed great store on players like that; men you can rely on. Anchor men. Jimmy was never brilliant. He never hit the headlines. But he was always there.

And what about little Bill Eckersley? He could stand under a table . . . but what a full-back. We had four world-class goalkeepers to choose from — Bert Williams, Sam Bartram, Ted Ditchburn and Gil Merrick. If any one of those had a bad game he knew what would happen next time out.

In 33 games for England I scored 30 goals and finished on the losing side just four times. I'm proud of that but I know I owe everything to the men who played alongside me.

The men I depended on; the men I respected.

CHAPTER SEVEN

The Lion of Vienna

I ALWAYS felt ten feet tall when they played the National Anthem before a big game overseas. I won 14 of my 33 caps abroad and that feeling never changed.

They usually played the home team's anthem first. That was the time to size up the opposition. In those days continental teams often used to wear numbers on their shorts as well as their shirts, so while their long, drawn-out anthems were playing I'd be looking along the line. Looking for the number five.

He was usually a big lad! 'By, Lofty, you're up against a big 'un today,' I'd think. Then I'd see him looking at me. You know how boxers try to stare one another out when they get in the ring before a big fight? Just the same.

When they played our National Anthem it would be shoulders back, chest out, try and look a couple of inches taller. Make sure he thinks I look a hard man, too. Still the eyeball to eyeball stuff. It was just like that on May 25, 1952. A day that will go down as my finest hour in an England shirt. The day they dubbed me The Lion of Vienna.

As we lined up for the start of that match I had even more reason than usual to give my opposite number, Austria's Ernst Ocwirk, rated one of the world's top defenders, plenty to think about.

It was the second match of our summer tour. Now in those days there was no pre-qualifying for the World Cup to occupy our time in the summer. There was no European Championship every four years. So those close-season tours meant a great deal. They might have called the games friendlies but that didn't mean they weren't important. They were a yardstick; our chance to see how we measured up against the continentals.

And England were still very much the team to beat. We were the nation who had given football to the world and now the world was ready to show us how much they had learned.

We started that summer tour with a game against Italy in Florence. The Italians have always been one of the top European nations and then, as now, a very tough proposition on their own territory.

It was a hot, humid day in Florence. The crowd was typically partisan. The Italians used all the tricks in their vast repertoire and a few more besides. We drew 1-1 but I didn't have one of my better days. Now a footballer is just like any other working man when it comes to knowing how he's played. If you've had a bad day at the office or the factory, you know it. You don't need the boss telling you. It's just the same with footballers. I knew I'd had a poor game in Florence. But we had, after all, drawn with one of the best teams in Europe.

So I wasn't ready for the reception I received in the Press. One newspaper proclaimed: Send out a Comet with Jackie Milburn on board. England needs Wor Jackie!

I always used to ring my wife in the evening when we were away on tour and when I rang on the day after our game in Florence the first thing she said was: 'You must have had a bad game, Nat, they're all saying Jackie Milburn should be flown out for the game against Austria next Sunday.'

Now I had a lot of time for dear old Jackie. I wish someone could fly him back on a Comet now. But I wasn't in any mood to have him take the England shirt off my back. I'd worked hard for it. And over the years I've always had a good working relationship with the Press. But I don't mind admitting that their reaction to my performance in Florence made me more determined than ever to bounce right back.

After the match in Florence we had a break in the lovely old city of Siena in the Tuscan hills. It was ideal. We were able to work out on the local pitch, wind down after the Italian game and prepare ourselves for Vienna. At that time, Austria fancied their chances a bit. They were rated the best side in Europe . . . at least they were in Austria! Some of us had other ideas. This match was billed as the unofficial championship of Europe. And waiting to cheer us on were some 30,000 soldiers who were based on the Rhine. They weren't all in the stadium when we kicked off. But it sounded like it. There was a lot of pride at stake.

I didn't do much for local honour when I gave England the lead in the first half from a Jackie Sewell pass. But it was never going to be easy and we found ourselves clinging on at 2-2 as the game went into the last quarter.

They could play a bit, those Austrians. But Ocwirk and the rest were just a bit too desperate to prove themselves. They were there to win at all costs. Instead of patiently waiting for their chance, they threw caution to the winds. That was their greatest mistake.

When they won a corner late in the game, almost everyone went up for it. I was left up front with just one defender to mark me. Gil Merrick caught the left-wing corner, spotted Tom Finney unmarked outside our box and threw it straight to his feet.

I set off. Now remember how I said Tom knew exactly how I wanted the ball, where and when? Well, he knew that day all right. His through pass left Austria's solitary defender standing and put me in the clear with only their keeper, a chap called Musil, to beat. I could hear the hounds setting off after me but I knew it was basically down to me and Musil.

Now some keepers are good in these situations. Bert Williams used to actually enjoy a man-to-man challenge. And it's never easy for the centre-forward either. People talk about 'missing with only the goalkeeper to beat.' But these chances are in many ways more difficult than the instinctive ones where you put the ball in the net without thinking about it. A good goalkeeper can make life very hard.

But Musil wasn't a good goalkeeper. I don't really think he knew what to do. He started to come . . . then he stopped . . . then he went back . . . hesitated . . . and finally came dashing out. My problem was not to hit the ball too early. I had to wait until Musil was totally committed. When he was, when he was right on top of me, I hit it. The next thing I knew Musil crashed into me and we collapsed in a heap. 'Bloody hell, Lofty. It's in!' It was Eddie Baily, first on the scene. I'd scored the greatest goal of my international career and never seen the ball go into the net. Tom joined in the congratulations. I had mixed feelings about it at the time as I was carried off on a stretcher. But after treatment from our trainer Jimmy Trotter I went back on . . . and what's more I hit the upright before the end of the game!

What a day! At the final whistle, hundreds of soldiers ran on to the field and chaired us off the pitch. It was a famous victory.

And what a night! We started off in the privates' mess, moved on into the sergeants' mess and finished up in the officers' mess. By which time some of us were decidedly unsteady on our feet.

At one stage of the proceedings I spotted the reporter who had called for the Comet to bring Milburn over. 'You won't be needing that Comet now,' I told him. He sent over a bottle of wine to help the party along. The next day I found myself hailed as *The Lion of Vienna.*

Many years later I went along to a Soccer evening in the little Lancashire town of Newton-le-Willows. It was given by the Earlestown FC Supporters Association. Highlight of the evening was a lecture by Tom Finney. Halfway through the evening, proceedings were halted by a special presentation . . . to me. I knew nothing about it. It was a trophy, a Lion mounted on a plinth. For these local Soccer fans it commemorated my glorious day in Vienna.

I felt very proud and very humble to receive that trophy. It remains one of my most treasured possessions.

CHAPTER EIGHT

A Pain in Spain

I'VE played in some hard games in my time. But there was never anything to match England's game against Spain in the Bernebau Stadium, Madrid, on May 18, 1955. There were times in that game when I wondered if they'd got our match mixed up with the tussle scheduled for later in the week in the nearby bullring.

It's a big place, the Bernabeu Stadium. One of the finest grounds in the world. A great football theatre. And on that day there were around 130,000 fans packed in. Not many of them were on our side. I suppose there might have been a few brave British fans in there somewhere. But in a hostile atmosphere like that no-one blamed them for not making themselves too conspicuous. We had no illusions about it, either. It was going to be tough and we knew it.

Quite how tough, though, we couldn't begin to guess. I've never known anything like it. We were kicked all over the field. And they singled out Stanley Matthews for special treatment. I don't think their left-back made one genuine attempt to go for the ball all afternoon. It's a wonder Stanley didn't break both his legs.

And I can now reveal that May 18, 1955 was the first and only time the great Sir Stanley ever lost his cool on a football pitch. That's how bad it was. Like I say, every time Stanley moved, this little left-back kicked him. Every time. And finally, as he wearily got to his feet after another session with the magic sponge, he turned to Roy Bentley and me and shouted: 'I've had enough of this chap. I could spit at him.' Roy, exasperated, replied: 'Spit at him! Never mind spitting at him, Stan. Bloody well kick him back.' He didn't, of course. And for Roy there was the consolation of getting the goal in the hardest-earned draw I've ever played in.

People often ask me how we coped with tactics like that. We simply had to turn the other cheek. It was no good getting involved in a kicking match. And for me there was always national pride at stake.

As we went out on to the pitch, our manager Walter Winterbottom would touch the white shirt and say quietly: 'Don't disgrace it lads. Play hard but play fair.' And we tried to live up to that. It wasn't always easy — particularly on days like Spain, 1955. But I always tried to think of myself as an ambassador for my country.

Yes, we had trouble with Latin sides over the years. They could all play the game but there was always something going on. I never relished playing against them.

In 1953, we went on a three-match tour of South America. Games against Argentina in Buenos Aires, Chile in Santiago and the world champions Uruguay in Montevideo. That tour was an eye opener for me on and off the field.

Like I say, these fellows could really play. I've nothing but admiration for their ball control and their skill. They're so easy on the ball. In Montevideo, one of their players ran 20 yards bouncing the ball on his foot as he went. Whether he'd have got away with that against Tommy Banks or Roy Hartle I'm not prepared to say . . . but it was a stunning piece of skill!

They played football, football, football all the time. No hopeful kicks upfield. I don't mind admitting that we often used to call on the old long ball upfield in times of crisis in defence. It's part of the English game; always has been. But the South Americans would never resort to anything like that. Even the centre-halves were comfortable on the ball and quite happy to play their way out of trouble. Even in their own penalty area. It was something completely new to me.

I was always used to the good old-fashioned English centre-half. The stopper. The Dave Ewings of this world. Bags of give and take and a handshake and a pint afterwards. But these boys were different class.

And that tour was also the first time I'd ever come up against a sweeper, the man lying in wait behind the centre-half. At home, if you were past the centre-half you were in the clear. The inside-forward or wing-half would push the ball through and shout, 'Off you go, Lofty. On your own.' But not in South America. There would be another man behind the main defender waiting to take the ball off your toes and start an attack at the other end. Yes, I learned a lot on that tour.

We knew all along that our opening game against Argentina was going to be hard. And the state of the pitch on the morning of the match did nothing to ease our troubled minds. It was rock hard. Absolutely baked solid after four or five weeks without any rain. Now I always used to like a bit of give in the ground. The heavier the better, really. So I wasn't happy. I remember saying to one of the lads: 'We could do with a drop of rain before kick-off.'

Well, we got it all right. And not just a drop. I've never seen anything like it. An hour before kick-off the heavens opened and when we walked out the pitch was like one of the Great Lakes. Players were slithering and sliding all over the place. Football was impossible.

The English referee Arthur Ellis was in charge and he gave it about 20 minutes before calling it a day. Nobody had any complaints . . . particularly England as we'd got away from Buenos Aires without being beaten.

We won the next game in Chile. A really enjoyable match. Mind you, they're all enjoyable on tour when you win and I had extra reason to celebrate with one of the goals in our 2-1 victory. Tommy Taylor got the other.

And so on to Uruguay. We knew it would be hard. It was. We lost 2-1. It would be nice to say we were unlucky. I had a shot early on that hit the post and rolled along the line before being cleared. But I don't honestly think it would have made much difference.

They were simply a better side. So fast, so smooth, so skilful. They were two up and coasting when Tommy Taylor got our goal. They gave the impression that they always had an extra gear. In this game, you've always got to admit if you've been beaten by a better side. I don't think anyone in our party would argue that Uruguay were better than us. The scoreline flattered us. It was up to us to learn . . . and try to do better next time.

That next time came sooner that we'd expected. In the 1954 World Cup in Switzerland. In our qualifying group we were drawn with Switzerland, Italy and Belgium. In those days you only played two of the teams in your qualifying group with the top two teams going through to the sudden death stage. We were due to play Belgium and Switzerland.

The first match against the Belgians produced eight goals. England got four of them, I got two of them and the fans were given a football feast. It was a good way to start the competition even though we hadn't really played all that well.

I missed the game against Switzerland but goals by Dennis Wilshaw and Jimmy Mullen gave us a 2-0 win so we were through to the quarter-finals. Switzerland went with us after winning a play-off against the Italians.

Waiting for us in the last eight were the Uruguayans. They had shown they meant to retain their crown by blitzing their way into the quarter-finals with some superb displays, including a 7-0 win over Scotland. I suppose it's fair to say that Uruguay and Hungary were the two outstanding sides in the world at that time.

But we weren't overawed. We'd played them 12 months earlier in South America and we knew what to expect. But, as so often in that 1954 World Cup, we failed to do ourselves justice. We never played to our full potential at any stage of the competition and the 4-2 win for Uruguay was a fair reflection of the match. Tom Finney and I got the goals.

So it was home sweet home for England. And there was no joy for our conquerors either. Uruguay were beaten by Hungary in the semi-final and then the Hungarians surprisingly lost to West Germany in the final.

Playing in a World Cup will always go down as a special thrill, though. It's the only time when all the world's greatest players are gathered together. I felt proud to be able to walk up to these men and shake them by the hand. Normally an international match is just a break from the daily First Division routine. Play at Wembley and then back to your club. Even on tour, there's a break between matches, usually a week in my day. But in a World Cup it's constant action. There's always a game of football going on. Football of the highest class, too. If you're not playing, there's a chance to go and watch another game; to watch the great players and learn.

Mind you, the Scots wouldn't have thanked us for watching that 7-0 defeat by Uruguay. Poor Willie Cunningham! He was an old pal of mine from games against Preston and internationals against Scotland and I felt for him that night. I don't think anyone or anything could have stopped that left-winger. Not even a bullet through the head. He would have kept on running.

It was a special atmosphere, Switzerland, 1954. The Italian team were staying in the same hotel as us and one evening I bumped into their centre-half, Ferrario of Juventus. He had given me a really hard time on that hot, humid day in Florence two years earlier. But he found an interpreter and we sat and chatted for over an hour. And not just about football either. Wives, kids, homes . . . that kind of thing. That difficult day in Florence was just a memory. Water under the bridge.

Get me to the church on time. December 6, 1947. Four hours later I was playing against Wolves at Burnden Park.

Newly wed . . . playing against Wolves four hours after my wedding.

King of the Castle. Alma and I take over at the Castle Hotel. Our reign didn't last long.

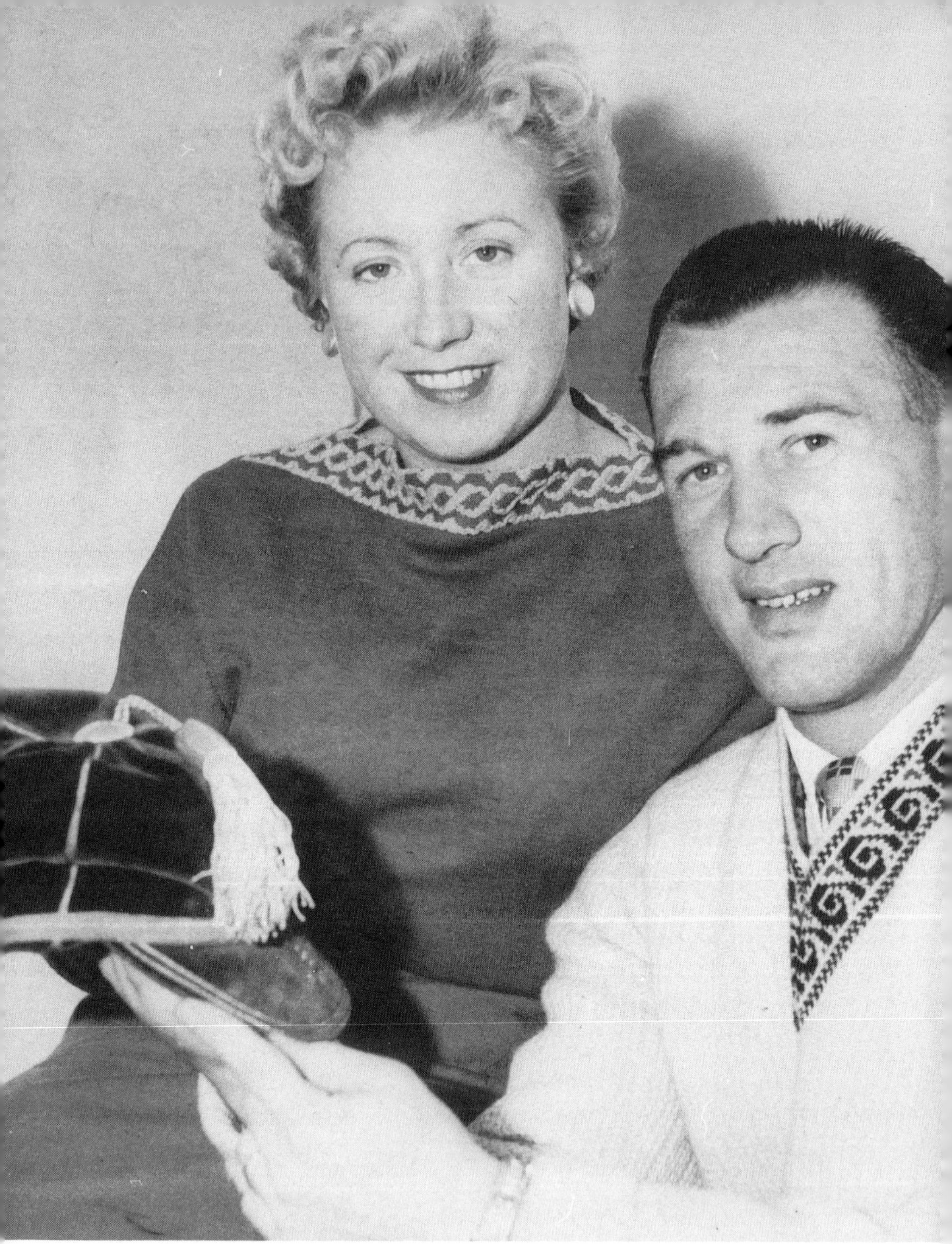

Alma and I celebrate another England call-up — and what do you think of the haircut?

Cheers! Opening night at St Mary's Social Club, Horwich. Alma and I do the honours.

The big match. Jeff leads the way in a family table soccer tussle.

The tragic scene of the Burnden Park disaster on March 9, 1946.

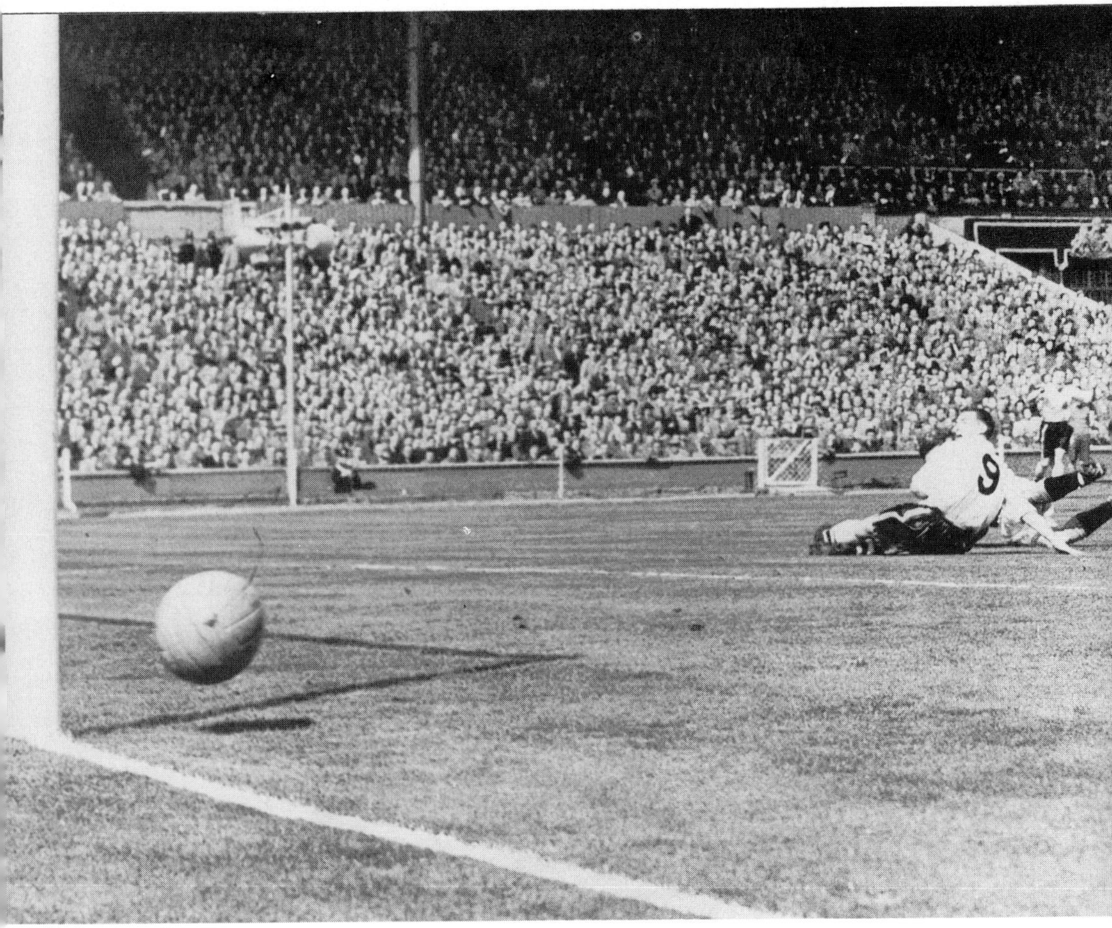

If only . . . I watch in despair as my second-half shot hits the post. That would have put us 4-1 up and not even Matthews could have pulled that back.

The class of '53. Back row (left to right): Bert Sproston (trainer), Nat Lofthouse, Johnny Wheeler, John Higgins, Stan Hanson, Matt Barrass, Ray Parry, Tommy Neill, Bill Ridding. Front: Eric Bell, George Higgins, Willie Moir, Ronnie Codd, Harold Hassall, Johnny Ball. On ground: Alan Beards, Ralph Gubbins.

1953 semi-final v Everton at Maine Road. I salute one of our four first-half goals — but we finished up clinging on for a 4-3 win.

CHAPTER NINE

Flower of Scotland

I'VE always said there are certain places that count in Soccer. Certain grounds that are part of a player's education, places where it means something to have played. A Wembley Cup Final. The World Cup. And I don't think an Englishman can really call himself an international player until he's played against Scotland at Hampden Park and at Wembley.

These games have a unique atmosphere. And I don't mean any disrespect to Northern Ireland and Wales when I say that matches with Scotland were the highlight of my career in the home internationals. I played against Scotland four times, twice at Hampden and twice at Wembley. I never finished on the losing side, winning two and drawing two. They were all special.

There is nothing to match the atmosphere at Hampden for a game against England. It is an unforgettable experience. When you walk out the noise is deafening. I suppose there are some English fans out there — but you wouldn't know it. The noise hits you in the pit of the stomach.

I know the pre-match ceremony is all part of a big game but at Hampden I couldn't wait to start moving, to work out the tension. The sight of 30,000 Scottish fans massed behind one goal was unbelievable. Hampden Park is a big place to be.

And I think you'll find the Scots think the same about Wembley. There was always that special atmosphere before the Anglo-Scottish match. And I enjoyed every minute of those four matches. If I had to pick one out it would have to be the 1955 match at Wembley . . . if the Scots will forgive me for reminding them. We won 7-2. It was Stanley Matthews' day. He laid on all seven.

Dennis Wilshaw got four of them, Don Revie one and I got the other two. Typical Matthews goals. All I had to do was be in the right place at the right time and boom! The Scotland left-back was a little fellow called Harry Haddock. Stanley ran him ragged that day. I don't think that Harry knew where he was at the final whistle. But all credit to him, he never resorted to foul play. He played it fair all the way through. Not like that Spanish chap in Madrid.

I don't think I've ever seen Stanley happier than he was after that match. He never showed much emotion and if you didn't know him you would have thought he had taken the whole thing in his stride. But I knew better. He was glowing. His eyes were shining. Totally elated.

I said earlier that I've always believed Stanley got more pleasure out of laying on a goal for someone else than from scoring himself. He proved it that day. To set up seven goals against Scotland at Wembley was something special . . . even for someone as special as Matthews.

In my first game against Scotland we won 2-1 at Hampden. I didn't score — Stanley Pearson got them both. But it was a good way to launch my career against them.

Before the Hampden game we would meet up at either Largs or Troon on the Wednesday. Tom Finney and I would travel up together. If we were at Troon the Scots were at Largs and vice versa. There was always something special about the build-up.

But that was all part of international Soccer. We weren't exactly treated like Royalty but it was the next best thing. Best hotels, best travel. Someone to carry the bags. Passports taken care of on overseas trips. On family holidays I never could get used to the idea of carrying my own suitcases!

And those matches against the Scots were always hard. I was up against men like big George Young, Willie Woodburn, Tommy Docherty, Willie Cunningham and the rest. Hard men. You could expect to take a few knocks. But there was never anything dirty. If you had a bruised ankle it was because you'd got a kick from someone going for the ball. On balance, he probably had a few bruises himself.

We'd shake hands after the match and they'd come into our dressing room. Big George would say: 'Come on, Lofty, get your coat on, we're going for a pint.' We'd played our best, done our job and now the fun could start. There was always a banquet in the evening. A really good do.

Ninian Park had an atmosphere all of its own too. My memories of those games against Wales will always bring back the fans singing 'Land of My Fathers'. To this day I can never hear them singing 'Land of My Fathers' without getting a lump in my throat.

I never played against Northern Ireland at Wembley. We usually played them at Goodison Park, presumably because it was easier for Irish fans to get to Liverpool. But Windsor Park, Belfast, was another ground with a very special atmosphere.

I thought my international career was over after the 1-1 draw with Scotland in 1956. I made an appearance as substitute for Tommy Taylor against Finland in Helsinki that summer — I scored a couple of goals, too — but by this time Tommy had more or less made the position his own.

Munich changed all that. We lost the best centre-forward of them all. And in the autumn of 1958, I found myself back in the side. I suppose our F.A. Cup victory that spring had something to do with it.

I said farewell to Wembley on October 22, 1958. England beat the Soviet Union 5-0 and I got one of the goals. I stayed in the side for the next match against Wales at Villa Park on November 26, a 2-2 draw. My final match for England.

I'd had a good run. Thirty-three games, 30 goals. I scored two goals in a match 12 times. I played with and against the greatest players of my generation. Playing for England was very important.

I've never met anyone who was actually glad not to be in the England side. It's the highest honour in the game, something we all cherish. But if I'm totally honest, I'll have to admit there was one day when I was, let's say, relieved to miss an England match.

The date? November 25, 1953. The opposition? Hungary. The result? One of the great landmarks of British — no, world — football. They beat us 6-3, the first Continental team to win on English soil. In doing so they set new standards for the domestic game.

We knew it was coming. There had been some pretty close shaves in the years leading up to November, 1953. In my first international, we had been held 2-2 by Yugoslavia. That was in 1950. The following year France also held us 2-2 at Highbury.

Austria, aiming for the top in the early fifties, drew 2-2 at Wembley in November, 1951, and just a month before the Hungarian game, we were held 4-4 by the Rest of the World. That was the closest of them all.

There was only a minute left for play when we were awarded a penalty when Stan Mortenson was brought down. As usual, it was all down to Mr Unflappable, Alf Ramsey. As usual, he took his time getting the lace pointing the right way. As usual he scored. Reprieved.

Ironically none of the Hungarian masters who were to teach us the lesson of a soccer lifetime played in that Rest of the World side. If the match had been played in December, not many other people would have had a look-in. I played in the match immediately before the Hungary game, against Northern Ireland at Goodison Park. I scored, too, but it was no great surprise when I was left out. I hadn't been playing too well.

The performance of Puskas, Hidekguti, Kocsis and the rest sent shock waves through the English game. Nobody did that to us at Wembley! But this lot had. And what's more they rubbed it in the following spring when they beat us 7-1 in Budapest.

I didn't play in that game either, so there was plenty of ammunition for dressing-room banter around the First Division grounds. 'They wouldn't have lost if I'd been playing!' I used to say. I won't repeat the answers.

CHAPTER TEN

Let's Call It Quits

THE only time I ever fell out with Bolton Wanderers involved an incident in a pub. No, don't get the wrong idea . . . it was my pub! But there was no danger of it being called The Happy Wanderer after all the trouble it caused me.

I was approached by a local brewery, Walker's, in 1957, asking if I fancied taking over The Castle Hotel in Bolton. It made a lot of sense. I was a big-name footballer. The pub was just across the road from my old school and in the area where I was brought up. Alma and I had reached the stage where we were thinking long and hard about what we would do when I finally had to quit football.

So I went along to the directors and asked for the go-ahead to become king of the Castle. They said No. What's more they gave every indication that if I wanted to go into the licensing trade I could forget all about playing for Bolton Wanderers. I pressed on and took over as landlord on May 29, 1957. I considered that I was looking after my own interests. I didn't know what the future held. I was 31 years old. For all I knew I might be injured in pre-season training and never kick a football again.

I needed to plan for the years ahead, and what better time to do that than when I was still skipper of Bolton Wanderers? This was an ideal chance for Alma and me to decide if keeping a pub was going to be the life for us. There was no guarantee that I would be kept on at Burnden Park in any capacity. It made sense to give it a go.

Needless to say the whole business received plenty of coverage in the local and national press. Wanderers were adamant I wouldn't be allowed to take a pub; I was equally adamant that I would.

I suppose, looking back, I wasn't really in the driving seat. There was no freedom of contract in those days and if Wanderers had dug their heels in I would have been out in the cold. There was no guarantee that they would have let me move on to another club, although there was some speculation that Blackburn Rovers were keeping a close eye on the situation.

Anyway, things never reached that stage. I like to think that good sense prevailed. I took over the pub and reported for pre-season training as usual. And the twin roles couldn't have done me much harm . . . we went on to win the F.A. Cup.

It wasn't as if I was rushing straight back from training to open the doors and pull pints. It was a big pub, with bar staff and a cellarman. I was more of a front man. In fact, because of my football commitments, it was Alma who put more time in than I did.

And if the 21 months we spent in the Castle proved one thing it was that we were not cut out for the business. It was just not our lifestyle and I was never happy about bringing up our two kids in a pub environment.

It had good moments, though. There was always plenty of banter from the customers and life was never easy if I'd had a bad game. I had to take my fair share of stick. But the regulars enjoyed telling their mates that the landlord wouldn't be behind the bar on Saturday . . . he'd be away at Wembley on important business for Bolton Wanderers!

I remember one day we received a visit from Henry Rose, the great *Daily Express* soccer writer. Now Henry was always larger than life, a really big name among the Press boys. And he delighted in having a go at the big-name players, me included, to boost the sales of the *Express.*

Anyway on this occasion he breezed into the vaults, bought a round for all the locals and then proceeded to discuss the ability, or otherwise, of their landlord as a centre-forward. Sadly it was Henry's one and only visit to the Castle. He was killed in the Munich air disaster along with several other journalists including Frank Swift, the great Manchester City goalkeeper of the thirties and forties.

We left the Castle in March, 1959. At least we knew that we wouldn't be spending the future behind bars but I was still no further forward in my long-term planning. Five months later I had to start giving the matter urgent consideration.

When I went over on my right ankle in a practice match at our Bromwich Street training ground it seemed like just another injury. I'd had plenty of those over the years, though thankfully nothing serious, and always bounced back as good as new. But I suppose that at 34 after 20 years in the game, time was running out. That ankle was never the same again. It was the beginning of the end.

I should have decided there and then to call it a day. When the ankle failed to respond to treatment I should have taken the hint and got out. But I suppose deep down I always wanted to give it one more chance. I've paid for it since. I've got arthiritis in both the ankle and the knee. It's just a hazard of the job, I suppose, and I know there are a lot of old players who are worse than me. Let's face it, your legs are for walking on, not twisting and turning, kicking and being kicked. That's bound to have some effect in later life.

As I say, I've done well, really. I've still got the pin in my shoulder from the injury that kept me out of the F.A. Cup semi-final back in 1958 but apart from a few twinges here and there I'm in reasonable shape. Apart from the brain, of course. That went years ago!

I had already decided that I would go out at the top. I had no intention of fading quietly away in the lower divisions. I had only ever played for Bolton Wanderers in the First Division. That's how I wanted it to stay. I sometimes used to look at players who had moved down into the Second and Third Divisions and wonder what they were doing there. I suppose they just didn't want to stop.

Perhaps, also, they couldn't accept that they were over the top. But I knew it. I knew when I started to lose that vital edge. The first thing that goes is that extra half a yard of pace. You don't quite meet those crosses that you would have put away a couple of years earlier. You're half a second late. And all of a sudden the centre-half is getting to the through balls before you.

And I had a certain Master Francis Lee alongside me in the Bolton side who had his own way of making the point. Franny was just breaking into the first team as I was trying to get over the ankle injury. We'd signed Billy McAdams from Manchester City and he was playing centre-forward with me at inside-right. Franny was on the wing.

He was only 16 but he could play a bit even then. And he was full of confidence. It was obvious he was going a long way. In one match we beat Manchester City 3-1. His crosses came over like bullets. Head high. You only needed a touch. Billy got one of the goals and eventually I got on the end of another cross to head another.

'Well done, Franny, nice ball,' I said waiting for the congratulations. 'About bloody time, Lofty, the number of crosses I've put over,' came the reply. There I was, over 20 years in the game, 33 England caps and a few goals to go with them, being put firmly in my place by a 16-year-old kid just starting out. I knew it was time to go!

But that was Franny. He always had an unshakeable faith in his own ability. It was no surprise to me when he went on to Manchester City and an England place. He belonged in the big-time. He joined a successful club under the guidance of Joe Mercer and Malcolm Allison. The old fox and the young lion. With men like Mike Summerbee and Colin Bell alongside him he helped City win the League title and the F.A. Cup and earned himself a regular place in the England side.

He played most of his football at Bolton on the right wing but I would always have put him on the other side. He was so dangerous when he cut in and let one go with that right foot. A great player, Franny, and a good pal. I always kept an eye on his progress after he left Burnden Park.

Mind you, that caused a bit of bother. Wanderers were in the Second Division by that time and Franny had already decided where he wanted to be . . . at the top. And he decided he wouldn't get there with Bolton. The club didn't want to let him go and it developed into one of those long-running transfer sagas. Franny got his way in the end. And he's never looked back.

Another young lad just coming through as I prepared to make my final bow was Gordon Taylor. Like Franny, he was a winger. Like Franny, a good little player. And like Franny, an intelligent lad. Gordon eventually moved on to Birmingham but even at Burnden Park he showed a keen interest in the PFA side of things, an interest that has now blossomed into his new career as Secretary of the Players' Union.

But as far as Nat Lofthouse was concerned the end was in sight. It seems odd to say it but I just sort of fizzled out. I carried that ankle injury until January, 1960, but it was no good. So I quit . . . or so I thought.

But just like a prize fighter always thinks he's got another fight left in him, I believed I might just be able to give it one more season. But they always say fighters never come back and I should have known the same applies to footballers.

My 'comeback' lasted a few reserve games and a couple of first-team outings before I suffered an injury to my left knee at Birmingham on December 17, 1960. And that was it. A very Happy Christmas! I'd had a good run.

I'd started my playing career at the bottom way back in 1939 and now, 21 years later, I was back at the bottom of the pile again. This time on the coaching staff. Wanderers wanted me to stay on and offered me the job of reserve-team trainer. And at Burnden Park the reserve-team trainer was responsible for mopping the dressing-room floor, cleaning out the toilets, washing out the baths, cleaning the boots and so on. How are the mighty fallen!

I'll be honest. I didn't fancy cleaning out the dressing rooms and all that sort of thing. I had, after all, been club captain and an international player. But when I took a step back and thought it over, there was never much chance of me turning the job down. It meant I could stay with Bolton Wanderers. And that, basically, was all I wanted to do. All I'd ever wanted to do.

CHAPTER ELEVEN

Management Man

TO this day I don't know why Bolton Wanderers wanted me to be their manager. What's more to the point, whatever persuaded me to take the job? I must go down as just about the worst manager in the world. I say that in all honesty. The job wasn't for me.

I've been associated with Bolton Wanderers for 50 years. Forty-eight of them have been happy. The other two I was manager. I took over from Bill Ridding in August, 1968. No doubt the club thought that as I had been a key player in the great days of the fifties I was the man to rebuild a side which had slid into Division Two. I had been chief coach alongside Bill for a year, so I was next in line behind him.

But I was never cut out to be a boss. I would have been an ideal number two. I could have been the Malcolm Allison to Joe Mercer — not as good a coach as Malcolm, though, I've always really rated him — but the man who trained the players, worked with them day in and out, shared the dressing-room banter.

I could have got players fit. I'd been doing that myself all my life. Nobody fitter than me ever played football. And I knew what made players tick, how to keep them happy on the training ground, how to build them up for matches and so on. Team spirit was always a crucial part of Bolton Wanderers' success.

I'd learned all about life on the training ground from George Taylor and George Hunt at Burnden Park. I knew all about man management from Walter Winterbottom. I'd talked tactics and training methods with men like Billy Wright, Tom Finney and Alf Ramsey. But what I'd never done was take the big decisions.

And basically that's what being a manager is all about. Your head is on the block. The buck stops in the manager's chair. You HAVE to make decisions that you know will hurt someone. I used to worry all night about how I would tell a player I was dropping him. If we won I'd go home and worry about whether we'd win again the next time out. If we lost I'd go home and go straight to bed.

I didn't mind the hard work. That's part of the job. A manager has to be out looking at players and watching matches up and down the country all week. Often there's only Thursday night and Sunday night at home. And even then there's always the telephone waiting to ring.

And on top of that I'd been one of the lads for so long. Everyone knew me at Burnden Park . . . but not as the boss. It was hard for the players to accept me. Perhaps if I'd gone to another club as manager and started from scratch as an outsider I might have done better. But that was not to be.

It was time for rebuilding. I brought in senior players like Charlie Hurley, John Manning and the England World Cup man Roger Hunt from Liverpool. I was looking for them to blend in with the youngsters. Wanderers had been relegated to Division Two in 1964 and they saw me as the man to bring back the glory days. It didn't work out. In November, 1970, they moved me upstairs as general manager.

I was glad. I was relieved to be out of the job. And if anything Alma was even more pleased about it than I was. If being a manager had been hard for me, it hadn't been much fun for her either.

So what is the secret? What have the great managers got that separates them from the nearly men? I doubt if even they know. It's a gift . . . just like scoring goals was a gift for Jimmy Greaves. But that old word 'respect' plays a big part.

Sir Matt Busby is the outstanding club manager of the post-War era and I have never met anyone in football who did not have the utmost respect for the man. I have never heard anyone say a bad word about him. But, like Walter Winterbottom, Matt didn't buy that respect, he earned it. He has a rare gift. He always seems to have time to stop and talk to people, even today when he's been out of the manager's chair for so long. He's recognised all over the world. He has charisma.

But he has gained the respect of the football world in a quiet, unassuming way. Matt knew from the start that a successful football club doesn't just depend on the eleven men out there on the pitch. It's a team effort from the President right down to the man who sweeps the terraces after a home game.

I'd like to bet that Matt knew every single person on the Old Trafford staff by name. Not just by sight, by name. I bet he went out of his way to chat to the ladies in the laundry, the men who operated the turnstiles, the groundstaff. Everyone. Because they're all part of the team. They all have a part to play.

And because Sir Matt went out of his way to spend time with them, they went out of their way to give a little bit extra to the club for his sake. And this atmosphere transmitted itself to the most important people of all . . . the fans. Sir Matt had a tremendous rapport with the fans and this had its own effect on the team.

He built some wonderful sides at Old Trafford. The post-War team of Johnny Carey, Jack Rowley, Stan Pearson. The Busby Babes. The European Cup side of Law, Charlton and Best. But they were just the men in the shop window. To Matt, the backroom staff were every bit as important.

Since he retired he has given help, advice and guidance to his successors at Old Trafford. In his role as President he's still very much the father figure, a man with an influential role to play in the affairs of a great club. But let's not forget that Sir Matt Busby is the man who made that club great. I often think they should re-name it Matt Busby United.

Managers are like players. If you want to find out how good they are, look at their record. You don't win Cups and Championships if you're a bad manager. Look at Brian Clough.

Controversial he may be. But he's a winner. And, like Busby, he's earned the respect of the men who play for him. People say Cloughie rules by fear . . . but you don't get players to win the big trophies if they're frightened of you. He's right up there with the great managers.

Clough has nothing to prove to anybody. He has done it all and he's still doing it. He took Derby County from the bottom of Division Two to the League Championship. Then he lifted Nottingham Forest out of Division Two and gave them two European Cups, a League Championship and two League Cups. Then he tore the whole thing apart and started again. His present side looks certain to be chasing honours for the next five years.

So what's his secret? Man management. Brian Clough knows how to get the best out of every player at Nottingham Forest. He knows exactly what makes them tick. Look at the time when his lad, Nigel, was injured and missed a couple of games. His stand-in did well.

So when Nigel was fit, what did Cloughie do? He made him wait. What an effect that must have had on the rest of the staff! Here was the manager's son having to wait his turn just like any other player. It can't be easy for Brian or Nigel at the club and a lot of people must have thought Cloughie was just going through the motions when he said Nigel would never receive preferential treatment. But no, here he was . . .

putting his money where his mouth was. Nigel had to wait. And wait he did. There were no special favours.

Brian is totally unpredictable. It's impossible to forecast how he'll react. Take his Littlewoods Cup Final victory over Luton. He stayed around long enough to commiserate with the Luton players and then set off for the dressing room, pausing to give the Forest fans a wave on the way. He left the glory to his players.

Lord knows what he did when he got into that dressing room on his own. Perhaps he yelled at the top of his voice: 'We've done it!' Perhaps he shouted and swore every rude word in the book. Maybe he calmly took off the old green sweater and tracksuit bottoms, put the smart blazer and flannels back on and waited in dignified silence for the conquering heroes to return. Who knows? Only Clough and his players . . . which is how it should be.

Clough is constantly at odds with officialdom because he says what he thinks. He has a love-hate relationship with the Press. He is never anything less than controversial. Only Clough would have got himself involved with those fans at the end of the Littlewoods Cup tie with QPR. I'm sure he bitterly regretted his actions but I'm equally sure it was a genuine, spur-of-the-moment attempt to preserve the good name of the club. He has taken Nottingham Forest into the big-time. He did the same for Derby County. He will never be the darling of the establishment, but for me he will always be one of the very finest managers.

Managers come in all shapes and sizes. There are the quiet ones like Busby and Bill Nicholson who just get on with the job, steer clear of controversy and let the players do the talking. And then there are the showmen, managers who seem to go out of their way to court publicity and live their life in the full glare of the television arc lights. Men like Ron Atkinson, Lawrie McMenemy, Terry Venables, John Bond. But I don't blame them if that's their style. They bring a new dimension to the game.

My only criticism would be if they couldn't do the job as well. It's easy to stand up and air your views on any Soccer matter under the sun. It's another thing to have a record that gives you the right to do so. And all four I've named have proved their pedigree.

Venables had the nerve to take on one of the biggest jobs in European football when he went to Barcelona. If you finish second there, you've failed . . . as Venables eventually discovered. But that was after he'd won the Spanish League and taken them to the European Cup Final.

Yes, I know his funds were limitless and his critics will say that anyone could have achieved what he did given the resources available. But if that's the case, why hadn't Barcelona taken out a mortgage on the Spanish Championship? Why hadn't they won the European Cup every year? They had to wait for El Tel.

Now he's taken on another big job at Tottenham and the critics weren't slow to pounce when he was struggling early on. But he'll survive. He had the confidence in his own ability and the nerve to go in for Paul Gascoigne, a player of the highest class. I'm sure he will take Spurs back to the top.

Like Venables, McMenemy was ready to take a chance when he moved to Sunderland. He had nothing left to prove at Southampton where he had taken a country club to an F.A. Cup victory and a regular place in Europe. More than that, he'd given Southampton style.

He also gave them big-name players. He persuaded Alan Ball to spend his later years at the Dell. And, above all, he brought Kevin Keegan back to British football from West Germany. What a master stroke! And what about that Press conference to announce Kevin's return? Lawrie produced him like a conjuror pulling a rabbit out of a hat. It was on the television news; it made the front pages as well as the back. In one moment, Lawrie had put Southampton up there with the big clubs.

All right, his move to Sunderland didn't come off. He went there as the new Messiah, the man those North-East fans had been waiting for to finally fulfil Sunderland's potential. And, like just about every other manager they've had at Roker Park, he didn't deliver the goods. But don't try and tell me that made him a bad manager. He had nothing left to prove when he went to Roker. He'd done it all at the Dell.

Bond and Atkinson were in tandem in Manchester for a while. Bond at Maine Road and Big Ron at Old Trafford. And while Bond's critics are right when they say he never won anything for City, his supporters will claim that his high-profile image and big-money signings at least helped to lift City out of the giant shadow of Old Trafford and took them to the F.A. Cup Final. And don't forget Bond's record at Norwich, another small club who were given a taste of the big-time.

Behind Atkinson's Mr Bojangles image lurk two things. One is a fine manager. The other is a genuinely nice guy, one of the best. His only failure at Old Trafford was his inability to bring the Championship back to Manchester United. That is the club's Holy Grail and a lot of good managers have perished in the chase. Ron among them.

But don't forget he won two F.A. Cups, produced a side that played flowing attractive football . . . and made a major contribution to the future welfare of United by signing Bryan Robson, a truly outstanding footballer and leader. Ron's record speaks for itself. Oxford, West Brom, Manchester United, Atletico Madrid. Spain must be the only footballing country in the world where a manager who takes a club out of the bottom three and into the top three in six months gets the sack. Ron has done well everywhere he's been.

We learned all about the other side of Ron Atkinson — the side the public never sees — here at Burnden Park when Mick Brown, our assistant manager and Ron's old sidekick at Old Trafford, badly injured a foot in an accident with a mowing machine. Ron did more than call us and Mick offering sympathy. He offered his services as a stand-in. Free of charge, of course. Needless to say, we accepted.

Look at the great sides and you'll find a great manager. Bill Nicholson and the Spurs double side of the early Sixties. Don Revie and his Leeds United side of the Seventies. I always saw Don as manager potential from our days in the England side. A great thinker and motivator. A man who was unswervingly loyal to his players. And then there's Liverpool.

Since the days of Bill Shankly, Liverpool have set the standards for English soccer. In Shankly, Bob Paisley, Joe Fagan and Kenny Dalglish they have produced four great managers. But more than that, Liverpool have established a system that is the envy of the football world. They have been winning things for nearly 30 years and there is no evidence to suggest that they won't still be winning things in another 30 years.

Continuity is the name of the game. When Shankly stepped down, his right-hand man, Bob Paisley, moved in and became the most successful manager in the history of English football. When Bob, an ex-Liverpool player himself, of course, decided it was time to go, Liverpool appointed his number two, Joe Fagan. More trophies followed.

And after Joe they once again decided to keep it in the family by promoting Kenny Dalglish. It was a surprise appointment. Kenny was still a player. He had no managerial experience. But he knew the system. He was already steeped in the Anfield tradition. Alongside him he had men like Ronnie Moran and Roy Evans who had served under Paisley and Fagan. And in the background there was Paisley himself. Looking back, it's hard to see how anyone could have had any doubts about Kenny succeeding.

All four have brought different qualities to the job but all four have one basic thing in common: a ruthless ambition to keep Liverpool on top. Kenny has been criticised because he doesn't say much. His Press relations are not the best in the world, let's face it.

But that's his style. What Kenny Dalglish has to say is said to his players. In private. I have never heard him criticise a Liverpool player in public. I don't suppose he ever will. But I wouldn't mind being a fly on the dressing-room wall sometimes. Kenny believes that what goes on between him and his players is personal. And that's how it will stay.

The important thing is that Kenny and the players know what is good for Liverpool Football Club. Everyone knows where they fit into the system. Everyone knows where they stand and what's expected of them. That's the Liverpool secret. A lot of people have tried to copy them, no-one has succeeded.

Kenny has set the standard for the young managers coming through. Players will always want to become managers; only a handful will get to the very top. One of the younger generation who has already been there is Howard Kendall, who won everything there was to win at Everton before trying his hand in Spain with Athletic Bilbao. He'll be back and he'll win more trophies.

Aston Villa's Graham Taylor is another man for the future. I like his honest, open approach to the job. He's sincere. He says what he believes and says it clearly. I'm very impressed with Dario Gradi at Crewe. Someone, somewhere will be giving him a chance in the big-time before long.

Dave Bassett has come in for some heavy criticism for the style of play he has brought to Wimbledon and now Sheffield United. Not, I hasten to add, from fans of Wimbledon or Sheffield United! The Bassett long-ball style may not go down too well with the purists but any manager who can take a club from the Southern League to the First Division in ten years must have something going for him.

People say it's not pretty. But it's pretty effective. He has developed a style of play that works. If people think it is so bad for soccer they should devise ways of beating it. In the meantime, why not give Bassett credit for what he has achieved?

But that's the problem with being a manger. You're always under fire from somebody. It must be the worst job in the world. I'd always had a wonderful relationship with the Bolton fans but that didn't stop them giving me a load of stick when I was the manager.

'If you don't win on Saturday, you want sacking, Lofty!' That kind of thing. And criticism during the game. Don't get me wrong, the fans have every right to say what they think . . . they pay our wages. But it's not easy when you're the man in the firing line.

You have to accept that it's part and parcel of the job and get on and work out with the board and the players how to put things right. Everyone is responsible for the team's performances. But it's the manager who's got to stand up and be counted.

How much better it would be if clubs gave managers a long contract that really was binding on both sides. That would take some of the fear out of the job. The manager wouldn't spend his life looking over his shoulder. He would at least be able to tell his players to go out and attack, win lose or draw; to be inventive, to give the fans something to shout about. To entertain. And that basically is what the game is all about, isn't it?

CHAPTER TWELVE

Thrown a Lifeline

I NEVER thought the day would dawn when Bolton Wanderers and I would part company. Burnden Park had been my life since I signed on as a schoolboy way back in 1939, and even though they had rightly decided I wasn't going to be the greatest manager in living memory, I thought I would always have a place at the club.

When the axe came it hit me like a sledgehammer. I was Chief Scout at the time. On June, 8, 1972, I was called into the boardroom. The Chairman, Jack Banks, was there with other directors. He was in tears. A big strong man, a builder, Jack was crying.

He just told me that the club had decided not to keep me on as Chief Scout. I had been relieved when they sacked me as manager. But this was different. This hurt. It came totally out of the blue and to this day I don't really know the background.

I was devastated. I don't really remember my reaction but I can recall walking out of Burnden Park, across the car park and down Manchester Road wondering how it could have happened to me. It was just a bad dream. Bolton Wanderers had been my life. Now I was no longer part of the furniture. It didn't seem true.

After moving out of the Manager's chair, I had been appointed General Manager. They brought in Jimmy McIlroy, the former Burnley and Northern Ireland inside-forward, as Manager and moved me upstairs.

I'm the first to admit this wasn't my kind of job either. As I've said, I was always a players' man. I could have been out there on the training ground and joining in the dressing-room banter. Instead I was office-bound. It just wasn't me.

Anyway, Jimmy McIlroy came and went, so did Jimmy Meadows, the former Manchester City and England full-back. The next man charged with the task of reviving Wanderers to their former glories was Jimmy Armfield, the Blackpool and England full-back and captain. A man, like myself, who had devoted his playing life to one club.

Jimmy inherited some good young players. Men like Peter Reid, Roy Greaves, Paul Jones, Neil Whatmore, Barry Siddall and Sam Allardyce, youngsters who had been coming through in my time as manager.

That side took Wanderers out of Division Three before Jimmy moved on to Leeds United to take over from Brian Clough after Cloughie's controversial 44-day reign at Elland Road. Leeds obviously saw Jimmy as a man to pour oil on troubled waters after Clough's turbulent reign following the departure of Don Revie to the England job.

He took the Revie side into the European Cup Final, where they were beaten by Bayern Munich, and then gradually rebuilt Don's team, replacing the old guard with men like Tony Currie, Paul Hart, Arthur Graham and Ray Hankin. He did a good job. But I often wonder if Jimmy wasn't perhaps a bit like me as a manager. I don't think he found it easy to take the hard decisions, the ones where people get hurt.

It was left to Ian Greaves, who had already taken another once-great club, Huddersfield, back into Division One, to do the same job at Burnden Park. They made it in 1978 after two agonisingly near misses.

Greavesie was a good manager. Underrated. I'd known him from the old Manchester United side that grew up after Munich. He was left-back in the team beaten by Bolton in the 1958 Cup Final. He always had a good relationship with his players. They could share a joke and a laugh with him but there was never any doubt who was in charge.

Under Ian, Bolton were so near but so far from becoming a First Division force again. He had a good side and he went out and paid big money for men like Len Cantello and Dave Clement to strengthen the squad. There was a good commercial set-up and the crowds came flooding back.

But somehow, agonisingly, it never quite worked out. In 1980, Wanderers were relegated again. Greaves left. And the downward spiral towards Division Four had begun.

I had been appointed Chief Scout under Jimmy Armfield, going out to look at players, run an eye over Bolton's future opponents and so on. Again, it was never really the job for me. But my sacking was still a bolt from the blue. I never thought I would leave Wanderers.

Of course, I couldn't keep away. There were things I could have said about the club. But I didn't. I never wanted to dig the dirt. That wasn't my style. It never has been. And Bolton Wanderers had, after all, given me a lifestyle I could only have achieved in my wildest dreams. I kept quiet.

There were opportunities for me away from Burnden Park. I did a bit of Public Relations work for a local supermarket chain, that sort of thing. And I don't recall missing a match. No, I wasn't going to stay away from my beloved Burnden Park just because I had been sacked. Sometimes I sat in the stand, sometimes I stood in the paddock. But I was always there to cheer them along.

And then the call came. It was from Derek Warburton, a director at Burnden Park. Would I pop down and have a chat sometime? Wanderers were looking for someone to run their new Executive Club, a place for members to go and eat before matches and have a drink or meal afterwards. There would be function rooms and the club would be open during the week for receptions, lunches and so on. They needed a front man.

I didn't have to think twice. I'd never been away from Burnden in spirit and here I was being given a chance to get myself involved in something really worthwhile again. To put something back into the club that had given me so much. The days when Bolton Wanderers — or any club for that matter — could survive purely on gate receipts had already long gone. This was a way of raising money and helping the club.

As a player I liked to think that my goals helped bring along the fans and keep the club going. Now I was given the chance to help the club by bringing in people and money.

The man behind the scheme was Alf Davies, the Commercial Manager at Burnden Park and, in my view, the best commercial man in the business. He's now at Headingley, Chief Executive of the Rugby League and Test Cricket grounds.

Alf was never slow to see an opportunity for raising money for the club and he obviously saw me as a man who could open doors for him in Bolton. And it was Alf who set up the Burnden Park Lifeline scheme which, I can confidently say, has kept Bolton Wanderers alive.

There's a weekly draw with big cash prizes. In the past we have also given away things like £35,000 villas abroad and foreign holidays as the big star prizes. We have 3,000 members each paying £2 per week. Half the money goes in prizes; the other half to Bolton Wanderers. So it doesn't take a lot to see how much Lifeline has meant over the years.

It became a role model for other clubs. Alf and I went round something like 40 Soccer and Rugby League clubs showing them how to set up a lifeline of their own. We went all over . . . and not just to the little clubs. No-one, not even the Manchester Uniteds, Liverpools and Evertons of this world, can exist these days without money-raising schemes like Lifeline.

I'm involved throughout the week. If there is a presentation to be made I go along and, hopefully, pull in a few more members, too. We've come a long way since Alf Davies and his commercial staff first started the ball rolling. We've brought in something like £1,600,000 and given away half of that figure in prize money. The rest has helped to keep Wanderers alive. We have a super commercial team. We're responsible for all the sponsorship at Bolton Wanderers . . . from the players' strip to the match ball, ground advertising and so on. Anything that involves raising money for Wanderers is our concern.

In the Executive Club we have 120 members. They pay £300 a year and this gives them club membership, a meal before the match and a seat in the stand . . . plus, of course, full use of the club's facilities. It's a place where people can meet for a drink and a chat, not just on match days but through the week as well.

In October, 1986, I was made President of Bolton Wanderers. It is a great honour but I see the job as much more than a title at the top of the club's letter headings. I'm still working flat out for Wanderers in any capacity. A football club has to pull together as a team . . . from the President and the Chairman right down to the lads who put the corner flags in before a match. Everyone at the club is important; everyone has a job to do which is vital for the club. And if everyone . . . officials, office staff, ground staff and playing staff . . . pulls together, then there's a good chance the club will be successful.

Bolton Wanderers is a big club. It's a First Division set-up. There aren't many grounds better than ours in Division One. That's where we belong. We have some of the best fans in the business. They're straightforward, honest, open and sincere. And the club belongs to them. Make no mistake about that.

If no-one turned up at Burnden Park on a Saturday there would be no more Bolton Wanderers. The same applies to Manchester United, Liverpool, Everton and the rest. The fans are the people who matter.

And I don't deny them the right to have a go at the players and the manager . . . even at me, sitting in the stand. They used to have a go at me on the field often enough so why should it be any different because I've changed jobs? It's only because they feel strongly about the club. Perhaps a chap has been getting some stick at work. 'Hey up, I see Wanderers lost again on Saturday, I don't know why you bother!' That kind of thing. He wants to be able to go in the next week after a 3-0 win and say 'We didn't do so badly this time, then!'

So if the side are two down after ten minutes he's bound to be upset. I don't mind . . . as long as the criticism is fair and as long as it isn't foul-mouthed abuse. Bad language is something we can do without.

It always amuses me when I hear the big cheer a player gets when he comes on as substitute. Perhaps the previous week the same player was booed off the park after having a stinker and then dropped on to the subs' bench. But here he is, running on to the field of battle to a roar of delight from the same fans who jeered him seven days earlier. But that's football. It will never change.

But can I just remind all you fans out there — not just Bolton Wanderers fans — that when you have a go at the manager or his players, think of the other people involved. They're just the men trying to do the business out there on the pitch. But everyone else at the club is responsible, too. And that's why everyone at a club must pull together as a team.

We have a hard core of around 5,000 fans these days, but if we can give them success that figure will soon rise. It's a chicken and egg thing, really. The fans will only come and watch a winning side . . . to find a winning side the manager needs to buy players . . . to raise money we need fans through the turnstiles!

I played for Wanderers in the First Division. In the years since I retired I've seen them slide down to the Fourth Division. Now, hopefully, we're on the upward march again. I'll never forget that night we were relegated from Division Three: May 17, 1987. We had finished fourth from the bottom but we found ourselves given a chance of survival through the play-offs.

We played Aldershot, who had finished sixth in the Fourth Division, in the first round of the play-offs. We lost 1-0 down at Aldershot in the first leg but I think most of us felt we could do enough at Burnden Park to go into the final. We couldn't. We drew 2-2. And Bolton Wanderers were down.

Aldershot went on to beat Wolves in the final and so earn a place in the Third Division. Two famous scalps from the great days of the fifties. No-one playing in my day could ever have dreamed that Wolves and Wanderers would one day be meeting in Division Four. Fortunately the following season we both moved up, without getting involved in the play-offs this time. Let's hope it isn't long before we meet again in the First Division.

We looked all set for a Wembley showdown in the Sherpa Van Trophy in the 1988-89 season. We met our old rivals Blackpool in the Northern Section Final. Wolves took on Torquay in the Southern Section.

Stan Mortenson and I led out the teams for the second leg of our match with Blackpool at Bloomfield Road. It was just like old times for both games . . . a big crowd and an exciting match. We won the first leg

1-0 and scraped through 2-1 on aggregate thanks to an extra-time penalty in the second leg. But Wolves, who won their first match 2-1 at Torquay, were beaten 2-0 at home. So it was the men of Devon who travelled to Wembley to meet us in our second Sherpa final in three years.

And good luck to them. Don't try to tell the fans of Bolton Wanderers and Torquay United that the Sherpa Van Trophy is a waste of time. And you'll find it just as hard to convince the players that their Wembley final isn't every bit as important as the real thing.

Because that's what Wembley means to players and fans alike. There are a lot of Soccer people who never get near the place. If the Sherpa Van Trophy gives those Third and Fourth Division players and fans a chance to make a dream come true, I'll back it all the way.

CHAPTER THIRTEEN

Name, Please!

I WAS only booked once in my career. Once in over 700 games for club and country. It's a record that I should perhaps be proud of but I still see that booking as a black mark on my career.

It was such a silly incident. I ran on to a through pass that put me in the clear and was just thinking in terms of another goal to add to the tally when the whistle blew. Offside. To prove it there was the linesman's flag. I don't remember what colour it was but I know I saw red. I picked up the ball and threw it at the linesman.

I regretted it immediately. But too late. As it looped through the air towards the linesman I remember thinking: 'Eh, Lofty, what do you want to go and do that for?' Yes, it was a spur of the moment reaction but I should never have done it. The referee was right to book me.

Funnily enough, the story has a sequel. At the end of that season we took a family holiday down in Bournemouth. I was playing on the beach at Branksome Chine with the kids when a little lad came up and said: 'Excuse me, Mr Lofthouse. May I have your autograph, please?' 'How did you know who I was?' I asked him. 'Oh, my Dad told me,' said the boy. Just then a chap strolled over and said: 'You don't remember me, do you, Nat? I was the linesman you threw the ball at that day you were booked at Burnden Park.' Talk about being brought down to earth with a bump.

My only booking . . . but generally bookings were few and far between in my day. There were no red cards and yellow cards, of course, and although the game was every bit as hard as it is today there weren't as many bookings. Why?

First I think that referees saw a booking as a last resort. They were reluctant to bring the book out. Like I say, there was always a lot going

Billy Wright . . . natural leader.

Stanley Matthews . . . incomparable skills. A perfectionist.

Matt Busby . . . charisma.

Roy Bentley . . . skilful.

Denis Law . . . explosive.

Heads I win . . . I beat Ronnie Burgess to score against Spurs.

Shooting star . . . and it's a goal against Sheffield Wednesday.

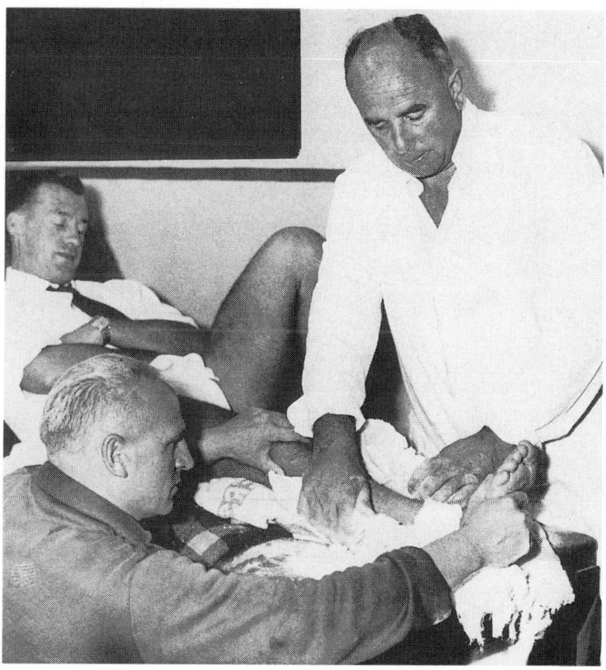

Lie back and think of England . . . Bert Sproston (left) and Bill Ridding treat an ankle injury as I dream of goals to come.

In the hot seat . . . I take over as Manager of Bolton Wanderers in August, 1968.

on but the referees would usually spot it and have a quiet word with the offenders during the run of play. OK, give a free-kick but don't haul a player out and give him a long lecture. Better to just say: 'Right, Nat, I saw that. Any more and you're in trouble.'

Then you knew you'd been warned. You knew exactly where you stood and you tried damn hard to make sure you didn't get on the wrong side of the referee again. You see, I've always said it takes 25 people to make a game of football. There are 22 players, a referee and two linesmen. If they all work together then the crowd will get their money's worth. If they don't you'll end up with a scrappy match.

It's basically down to fair play all round. If you know you touched the ball last, you don't appeal for the throw in your favour. If you know the ball was a yard out of play you don't argue when the linesman gives a throw-in. And the referee and linesman must apply the same laws of give and take.

And the second reason there are more bookings follows on from this. Too many players these days try to con the referee. How often do you see a player go down as if he's been hit by a double decker bus, roll around in agony and then lie still, waiting for the smelling salts? Half a minute later he's running around like a deer.

But there's every chance that the player who made the tackle has been booked. Yes, players will commit fouls, players will mistime tackles. But I think it's fair to say that in a lot of cases they will only be booked if the referee thinks the opponent has been hurt. Is it a habit our players have picked up from the Continentals and South Americans? If so, it's time they got out of it. In my day you tried to hide it if you were hurt. You didn't want the centre-half to know he'd got to you.

There have always been bad boys. There always will be. There will always be players who overstep the mark. I had them in my day and we have them today. There are times when players go too far. But there's a referee out there whose job it is to make sure the bad boys are kept under control.

And if the referee decides a player has to go, then there is a disciplinary procedure to follow. He will be suspended. If he does it again, he will be banned again. And so on. Eventually a player can — and should — be suspended *sine die.*

The clubs have a duty, too. To the fans and to the game as a whole. They must make sure that they root out the persistent offenders. It's no good the F.A. slapping a long ban on a player if his club only pay lip service to the disciplinary code. They should have their own code of conduct, too. And they should stick rigidly to it.

But like I say, the key figures in the whole business are those 25 men out there on the pitch. They can make or break the show. And give the players a good referee and you'll usually get a good game. The Salford referee Neil Midgley is a good case in point.

He was in charge of a game between Liverpool and Wimbledon recently that had all the makings of a really tough one. Wimbledon's F.A. Cup Final win over Liverpool hardly endeared them to the football purists and there was a lot of pre-match talk about trouble brewing.

But nothing happened. Why? Because Neil Midgley was in command. The players knew it and they responded. Vinny Jones went in just as hard as ever and when he committed a foul he was punished. But there it stopped. I lost count of the number of times I spotted Midgley having a word here and there with players who were getting steamed up. In doing so he took the steam out of the situation and helped to create a good, hard game of football.

It's a difficult job and the really top-line referees are worth their weight in gold. Mind you, men like Arthur Ellis in my day didn't have to put up with the action replay camera covering their every move. It's always easy to be wise after the event and there are times when the pundits go too far with action replays. Let's face it, the referee has to make a split-second decision on an incident as he sees it. If he had a portable camera to give him an instant replay he might make a different decision. But he hasn't. He gives his verdict honestly and dispassionately. And there will be times when he will be wrong. Just as players and managers are wrong . . . and even television critics!

But don't run away with the idea that I regard the action replay camera as an entirely bad thing. Far from it. Proper use of the action replays could make life a lot easier for the disciplinary commission and, in its own way, help to clean up the game.

Action replays are already widely used to decide whether or not a player committed an offence. It's no good a player proclaiming his wide-eyed innocence when there's a film revealing all the grizzly details. But by the same token, the player must be allowed to provide crucial film evidence to prove his innocence or justify his actions.

No-one has yet proved conclusively that there is a link between trouble on the pitch and trouble on the terraces. I don't think they ever will. But it's up to the players to make sure that they do not incite the fans.

A lot of people criticise the way the modern players celebrate a goal, all this leaping about and hugging and kissing. They believe this causes trouble in the crowd. I disagree. Players have always celebrated a goal.

When I scored I used to run back to the centre circle as fast as I could. Arms raised. Why? I don't know. At the time I didn't really know I was doing it. I was just overjoyed at scoring a goal. That was my job; what I was there for. I was helping Bolton Wanderers to win. No wonder I was pleased.

And it's basically no different now. The players are a bit more exuberant but that's all. Why shouldn't they celebrate with the fans? But I would add one word of warning to those players: only celebrate with your own fans. None of this gesturing at the opposition. That will cause trouble.

Dissent is another problem. Players have always had the odd niggle with the referee. It's human nature. But a good referee will stop things getting out of hand with a joke or a short, sharp reply. What we must stamp out is this mass protesting where virtually a whole team surrounds the referee. They must know they're wasting their time. All they're doing is setting a bad example to the fans and young players. Footballers, like anyone else, must accept authority.

Trouble at football grounds is something we can all do without. How did it start? Where did the hooligans come from? Search me. In my day there was never any trouble. You hardly saw a policeman inside the ground. Yes, there were arguments among rival fans but it was basically good-natured stuff.

And there was very little bad language. The fans themselves would see to that. If someone started swearing you could guarantee people nearby would call out: 'Hey do you mind, there are women and kids over here.' And the swearing would stop. Now you get a whole kop chanting and swearing together. Why? Where have we gone wrong?

If I could answer that I'd probably be Prime Minister, not President of Bolton Wanderers. But I'm convinced that it's a symptom of the society we live in. Football is just the vehicle for these hooligans. They're not football fans. They're troublemakers who use the game to create trouble. If it wasn't football, it would be something else.

Thirty years ago the football match was a day out. A group of friends would go off to the match, have a pint and a pie beforehand and home for tea . . . probably with the Saturday night Soccer papers. If you didn't turn up your pals thought you weren't well. Next week, an away trip.

Or maybe two fans would take their wives along to an away match — particularly to a place like Blackpool. The girls could look round the shops or walk on the prom while the men went to the match. Then a drink and a bite to eat on the way home. A grand day out. Blackpool v Bolton used to attract 25,000 or 30,000 to Bloomfield Road. Now they're lucky to get 6,000.

But don't blame football. By and large, hooliganism inside the grounds has been eliminated. Yes I know there are outbreaks of trouble, but for the most part the clubs have got it under control. It's outside the grounds where we have the problems, at the stations, on the streets, in the city centres. That's where the government and the police have got to act.

And I don't think for a minute that introducing an Identity Card scheme for football fans will help in the slightest. The hooligans won't go away. But the true football fans will. Or should I say those that we have left. If everyone in the country had to carry an ID card, fair enough. They would have to produce it wherever they went . . . football, cricket, golf, the cinema, the theatre. But why pick on the football fan?

Why should he have to endure extra time queuing outside the gates while ID cards are checked? No doubt getting wet at the same time. Big clubs are talking about putting back the kick-off by half an hour just to get the fans in . . . provided they turn up half an hour earlier than usual. Do you know what those fans are going to do? Stay away. If you went to a shop to be told how, when and where you could spend your money, what would you do? Go to another shop. It's just the same with football. The fans just won't bother going.

Away from the grounds, it's up to the police to keep the hooligans under control. At the grounds, the fans should be able to get into the ground quickly, not kept hanging around. That's how tempers get frayed, and bad tempers cause trouble. Once inside the ground they should be segregated and kept under strict control. For the most part that is now being done.

I went along to the House of Lords in February, 1989 to register football's protest over the ID card scheme along with Tom Finney, John Charles and Ivor Allchurch. The message is simple. ID cards won't beat the hooligans. They'll go elsewhere. But those same ID cards could well sound the death knell for football as we know it.

CHAPTER FOURTEEN

The Show Must Go On

I DON'T suppose the man who decided that money is the root of all evil was thinking about football when he coined the phrase. But he wasn't far off the mark. A lot of the game's problems date back to the abolition of the maximum wage back in 1961.

Let me say here and now that if I was playing today I would be in there with the best of them demanding the top money. A player only has a limited lifespan and it's up to him to make as much out of the game as he can while he's still around. There's nothing wrong with that.

If there had been freedom of contract in my day I don't suppose I would have been a Bolton Wanderers player for all those years. When my contract was up I would have been in there asking how much they were prepared to pay. If I could have got more elsewhere then I would have been off. A player has his wife and family to think about. And his future.

The trouble is, though, that only a handful of clubs can afford the best players. All the stars are being cornered by a small elite group. Even big-city clubs like Newcastle are unable to hang on to their stars. Look at some of the men they've sold. Players like Peter Beardsley, Chris Waddle and Paul Gascoigne. All high-class performers. The top players want the top money and they're prepared to go anywhere to get it.

And as the rich clubs get richer, so the poor clubs get poorer. The outlook is decidedly bleak for the little clubs these days unless they can unearth a jewel like Scunthorpe found in Kevin Keegan. For the rest it's a question of relying on fund-raising and so on.

When I retired I was earning the top wage of £20 a week plus £2 bonus for a win and £1 for a draw. I didn't consider myself badly off and I think a lot of players felt the same. If the F.A. had met the PFA halfway and come up with a realistic wage, then I think strike action would have been averted and a lot of today's financial problems avoided.

In my playing days we had Bolton, Blackburn, Preston, Blackpool and Burnley all within 30 miles of one another, all in the First Division and all doing well. Small-town clubs with a reputation for building their own sides. Look at them now. Only Blackburn are still around in the Second Division and they've done their time in the Third.

The smaller clubs either have to sell to survive or, if they produce players capable of bringing back the good days, are forced to let them go to the clubs who can pay out the big wages. I don't say it's impossible for a club like Bolton to get back into the First Division but it will take time . . . and money. And how do they get that money? Selling players. It's a vicious circle.

And I blame money for the lack of fun in the game today. Soccer is too important to be fun. We used to have people like Len Shackleton who was famous for his showmanship. Shack would play his party tricks and have the fans howling with delight. But he was still a highly effective player. And our own Tommy Banks would always find time for a chat with the fans in the paddock. 'Phew, that was close,' he'd say if the other team had nearly scored. Or 'We were lucky to get away with that one'. The fans loved him for it. I used to have a bit of byplay with them myself and I remember Stan Mortenson always joined in the fun if something amused the fans. You could afford to in those days. There was less emphasis on results.

Can you imagine how Shackleton would be received today? 'Hey, cut it out. It's my job you're fooling around with out there.' That's what his manager would say. Results are everything now. It's no good a manager turning round and saying how entertaining his team is. They have to win as well. Showmen are immediately suspect because people think they don't take the game seriously enough. Perhaps the problem is that too many managers take the game too seriously.

One of the few real showmen around these days is the Liverpool goalkeeper Bruce Grobbelaar. He's always ready with a smile and a wave to the fans; he'll play the odd trick, wear a silly hat, do a handstand, that kind of thing. And it hasn't stopped him from becoming one of the very best goalkeepers in the game.

In fact, over the years I suppose goalkeepers have always been crowd pleasers . . . and still contrived to keep Britain on top of the world in goalkeeping standards. I've seen some of the best from close quarters. Too close in some cases . . . and not just for the keeper. I've come across more than my fair share of keepers who knew my reputation and were prepared to 'get the first one in'.

I often used to get a thump on the back of the head as I went for an early cross and a reminder from the keeper: 'There's more where that came from, Lofty!' But it didn't stop me going in just as hard next time around.

The great Frank Swift set the standards for keepers before and after the Second World War, yet he would fool around with the best of them. Swifty often used to make an acrobatic flying dive that had the crowd roaring . . . even though he knew full well the ball was going a couple of yards wide. And those enormous hands! He's the only person I know who could catch a football in one hand. Then he would hold it over the centre-forward's head, just out of reach. The crowd loved it.

Big Sam Bartram, the Charlton keeper, was another larger-than-life character. Like a lot of goalkeepers Sam enjoyed the centre-forward's challenge. He was never averse to mixing it . . . but all in the best possible spirit, of course.

I remember once playing Charlton at the Valley when Big Sam was in goal. I thought I was through as I charged after a pass from our own half but I reckoned without Sam. He came racing out of his penalty area and as the ball bounced coolly headed it over me, nipped round behind me and set an attack in motion. As he passed me on the way back to his goal he gave me a wink as if to say, 'You didn't think I could do that, did you?' I do now.

There were always plenty of top-line keepers around. Men like Bert Williams, Gil Merrick and Bert Trautmann. Then along came our own Eddie Hopkinson, Alan Hodgkinson, Ron Springett and . . . Gordon Banks.

If I had to name the greatest goalie of them all it would have to be Banks. He had everything, the complete goalkeeper. He was good on the deck and in the air. His anticipation was excellent. He knew when to come for a cross and when to stay. He was brave. He could catch, he could punch. Brilliant. The best there has ever been.

And Peter Shilton isn't far behind. Between them he and Banks have monopolised the England jersey for 25 years and, remember, Peter had to fight off the challenge of another world-class keeper, Ray Clemence, who won 61 caps himself. Think how many caps Shilton would have collected if Clemence hadn't been around to stake his own claim for a place.

Shilton is a fitness fanatic. He has to be to still be playing top-line Soccer at the age of 40. He's a complete professional and deserves all the honours that have come his way. He will take some replacing. Even so there are one or two snipers around who say he's over the hill. He keeps proving them wrong. His saves in one of England's World Cup qualifying games in Albania would have done a 23-year-old proud.

Neville Southall, the Wales goalkeeper, is in the same class. Southall says his aim is to play on until he's 45 and I see no reason why he shouldn't. A top-line keeper must train just as hard as an outfield player but of course he doesn't suffer the same wear and tear during a match. An outfield player rarely stays the course until he's 40 but a keeper can go on for longer.

The great thing about Southall is his ability to maintain the highest standard week in and week out in the First Division. He hardly ever makes a mistake. Come to think of it, when he does it's usually back-page news. That's a measure of the man.

I could never have been a goalie. What a job! Make one mistake and you can lose a match. A centre-forward can miss out all afternoon but if he's around to put one away in the 89th minute and win the match he's a hero. Keepers come in all shapes and sizes but I've no doubt the Football League produces the best in the world. Why?

Well, for a start, continental goalkeepers are very much a protected species. They don't expect to be hit if they go for a cross. They aren't used to a challenge from the centre-forward. So that's one area in which they're bound to be suspect. By the same token, centre-forwards were never encouraged to challenge the keeper anyway. As I've said, Walter Winterbottom always used to warn me off and in many ways that affected my game as an England player. Challenging the keeper was an integral part of my make-up as a player and it wasn't easy to adapt to new techniques at the highest level.

And then foreign defences are so often much tighter than ours and a keeper doesn't have anything like as much to do. While it's true that a sign of a great keeper is his ability to pull off a vital save after he's been doing nothing all afternoon, it's also true that a keeper who doesn't have many saves to make doesn't make many blunders. Whatever the reason, British is best . . . and my old pal Harry Gregg will always rank with the greatest.

Harry is open, straight, honest and brave . . . remember how he went back into the Munich air crash to help rescue his team-mates? That speaks for itself. And he's also very funny. He would always be ready with a quip during a game. He'd go for a 50-50 ball and if I came out unscathed he'd shout: 'Missed you that time, Lofty, but I'll be waiting!'

Mind you, his plan backfired badly on one occasion. As you know, Harry vowed awful revenge for my challenge against him that gave us our second goal in the 1958 Cup Final. He always claims I turned him into a religious man because he used to pray every night for a chance to get even with me.

Well, that chance came just before the end of my career. We'd just signed Billy McAdams from Manchester City and he was wearing the number nine shirt that everyone had come to regard as my personal property. I was in number eight. Anyway as this cross came over, Harry came out like a fighting bull . . . and down went McAdams, number nine shirt, Harry and all. But the smile was quickly wiped off Harry's face when he picked himself up and looked straight into the eyes of one Nat Lofthouse. Poor old Billy! I don't think he knows what hit him to this day . . . or why. But Harry and I have had many a laugh about it since.

CHAPTER FIFTEEN

1966 And All That

I'VE always said that England's victory in the 1966 World Cup was the best thing that happened to our game at international level. No doubt about it. Alf Ramsey said we would win the World Cup. We did. Our standing in the world game has never been higher.

Alf changed the face of soccer. From that day in the summer of '66, the wingless wonders became fashionable. Alf Ramsey's 'English' game was copied all over the world and that victory was the platform for many of the European successes that followed until our teams were banned after the Heysel Stadium disaster in 1985. And four years after our 1966 triumph, England were still the team to beat in the 1970 competition in Mexico.

But I hope Alf will forgive me for saying that his World Cup triumph was the beginning of the end for the domestic game as I had known it since I joined Bolton Wanderers way back in 1939. I'm certain that I could never have been part of Alf's England set-up. I needed wingers . . . just ask Tom Finney and Stanley Matthews!

And while Alf's system worked miracles for England, with players of the highest quality in the side, it was a different story in the Football League. All over the country managers jumped to copy the system that had beaten the world . . . but playing 4-3-3 in front of 100,000 at Wembley with men like Alan Ball and Martin Peters in the side is one thing. Trying to make the system work on a cold February afternoon at Crewe is another matter altogether. And with the departure of the wingers, a lot of traditional entertainment went out of the game.

English fans had been brought up on the idea of attacking football. And a key part of that game was the presence of two wingers going to the by-line, putting over the cross and hoping the big centre-forward would be there to meet it. It was a fundamental part of our game. But Alf changed all that. And for a while fans were happy to bask in the reflected glory of that World Cup win . . . until it dawned on them that the product they were paying for every Saturday afternoon was, for the most part, not such good fun any more.

Instead of wingers we had attacking full-backs. George Cohen set the trend that men like Terry Cooper were quick to follow. Nowadays there's talk of teams reverting to the use of wingers. But how many teams really do go out and play with two genuine wingmen? They don't call them wingers any more. They're 'wide players'. And there's rarely more than one 'wide man' in a side.

It's a shame. I often wish that someone would go out and play the old 2-3-5 system. Just for the hell of it. I wonder how modern defences would cope with it. How would they handle two old-fashioned wingers, two inside-forwards and a centre-forward? Would they funnel back in alarm and think: 'Hey up, there's five forwards here and only four of us. What do we do?' Or would they say: 'Never mind this lot, let's see how their two wing-halves handle our four-man midfield!'

Interesting. I don't say for a minute that the old-fashioned system would come out on top. But given some of the great wingers I played with in my day, I fancy they would cause their fair share of problems. Perhaps one day some manager will give it a go.

But don't run away with the idea that I don't have the greatest admiration for the modern generation of footballers. I do . . . right back to the 1966 World Cup side.

The players are fitter now than they've ever been. The facilities available to them are superior. We had one man, Charlton's Jimmy Trotter, with the England party acting as trainer, physio, bag man . . . everything. If it was going to be muddy, we'd ask Jimmy to change our studs. He'd organise what we wanted for pre-match lunch. Fish, eggs, steak or whatever. He'd lay out the kit. If we got a knock he'd be out on the pitch with the magic sponge.

What a difference today! When England go abroad they take their own physio, masseur, chiropodist, dietician. They even take their own potatoes sometimes! All this goes back to Alf Ramsey's attention to detail. Today's players are reaping the benefits at both club and international level.

And I don't go along with the idea that the modern player lacks dedication. These facilities are available to him and as far as I can see he makes the most of his opportunity. There will always be one or two who don't behave. Players fell by the wayside in my day, too. But the vast majority are good professionals. Over the last 20 years or so there have been some marvellous players in the British game.

Take Alf Ramsey's team. I've already said that Gordon Banks is the best goalkeeper I've ever seen. The full backs, George Cohen and Ray Wilson, were outstanding. In fact, Ray's blunder in the Final that gave West Germany their first goal was just about the only mistake he ever made in an England shirt. We had to pinch ourselves to make sure we weren't dreaming. Between them they had Jack Charlton, so solid and dependable and now an interational manager of the highest pedigree, and Bobby Moore, one of the greatest readers of the game I have seen and a natural leader.

Nobby Stiles and Alan Ball were the nearest thing to old-fashioned wing-halves you could want. I often wondered what would have happened if you'd put them in a cage of lions. I'm not sure who would have come out on top. Their tackles could certainly bite!

And with them in the middle of the field were two of the greatest players of the generation. Alf once described Martin Peters as being ten years ahead of his time, a remark that Peters had to carry for the rest of his career. If he had a bad day — and we all have them — no-one let him forget those words.

But Alf was right. Martin's positional play and anticipation were uncanny. He was still playing at the very top ten years after our World Cup victory and he was still a highly effective player. And what about Bobby Charlton? One of the finest players we have ever produced. A magnificent ambassador for Soccer and for England on and off the field.

Those two goals he scored against Portugal in the World Cup semi-final are something I will never forget. Bobby was a magnificent striker of the ball with either foot. He could hit the target from any distance. And yet he wasn't primarily a goal scorer. That was almost a by-product; just part of an all-round game that made Bobby the key figure in our World Cup success and in so many triumphs at home and in Europe for Manchester United.

Up front, Alf had Roger Hunt and Geoff Hurst . . . and not Jimmy Greaves. If you'd asked any England fan before that World Cup if we would win without Greaves, he would have laughed you out of court. Greaves seemed indispensable. He was an instinctive goalscorer. He was like a flash. Six yards out, his close control was out of this world. He probably couldn't tell you how he got himself into those scoring positions but he knew where to be and when. He made goalscoring look simple. As a finisher he was in a class of his own.

Yet Alf left him out in favour of Hunt, whom many people wrongly regarded as a workhorse, and Hurst, relatively untried at the highest level. And what happened? Hurst scored a hat-trick in the World Cup Final and went on to establish himself as one of our premier post-War goalscorers. Alf was right again.

What, I wonder, would Alf have made of two more great 'naturals' of that era? Denis Law and George Best. Together with Bobby Charlton, Law and Best brought a new golden era to Manchester United and Matt Busby. They were outstanding players and, above all, outstanding personalities. Their very presence on the United team sheet was enough to put 5,000 on the gate. And rightly so.

The Old Trafford fans christened Denis 'The King'. He was, too. A marvellous player. I haven't seen many better. He was so quick, so alert and so deadly in front of goal. Denis never stopped running. Bobby Charlton would boom in one of those 20-yarders and he would be in there after it. Ninety-nine times of out 100 Bobby's shot either went in, flew wide or the keeper saved it. On the 100th time, the keeper fumbled. Enter Denis Law. We lost count of the number of goals Denis scored from that range. People called it instinct. Perhaps it was to some extent. But it was also hard work.

On the field Denis was arrogant, cocky, abrasive. And he wasn't play-acting. That arrogant streak was a crucial part of his make-up. The fans loved it. He loved the fans. And yet away from the limelight he was quiet, withdrawn, a family man.

If only George Best had been the same! On the field Best was the best. I loved to watch him. I would gladly make a special journey just to see George play. Many a Dad would take his lad to watch United just to see Best in action. On the field he was an inspiration to a generation of football fans and young footballers.

It was a pure, natural talent. George would do outrageous things. He would score goals that players before or since would not even contemplate. What a shame that he robbed millions of people of endless hours of delight by leaving the game so early. Perhaps, with all the publicity and adulation he received, it was inevitable that he would press the self-destruct button. And I always think that George would have drifted away even earlier without Matt Busby in the background. But let's not criticise him for his lifestyle off the field. Let's remember his genius on it. We will probably never see his like again.

Law, Charlton, Best . . . the big-name trio in a side that also boasted the talents of Nobby Stiles and Pat Crerand, a man who could almost make the ball talk. No wonder they gave Busby the trophy he always dreamed of, the European Cup.

In some ways that United side was the last team to throw up such a great collection of indivuduals who are remembered for their own skills. Law, Charlton and Best fitted into the framework of a great side, yes, but they are primarily remembered for their own superb individual skills, too. That was the genius of Busby, blending such talents into a team without reducing their individual flair.

Since then we have had many great teams who have done great things at home and in Europe. But for the most part it's the teams we remember, not so much the players. Don Revie's Leeds was a great football machine with some superb individual players like Billy Bremner, Johnny Giles, Eddie Gray and Allan Clarke. But they will always be remembered as a great TEAM above all else.

Liverpool, over the years, have included some wonderful players but overall we talk about the Liverpool machine rolling on. The players are very much the component parts. They change — but the pattern doesn't. Why should it when it's so successful?

Bill Shankly unearthed a diamond when he paid Scunthorpe United £30,000 for Kevin Keegan, who immediately won himself a place in the hearts of the fans who stand on the Kop. When he left, along came Kenny Dalglish and Graeme Souness, the supreme professionals. Now when we talk of Liverpool, we talk of John Barnes and Peter Beardsley, two players who surely have a key role to play in England's future, too.

Like Best, Barnes can create something out of nothing. His critics say he's lazy, that he doesn't contribute enough to the overall effort. But he wouldn't be in the Liverpool team if that was true. Barnes can be devastating. His footwork is superb. He can take men on, he can make goals and he can score them.

So can Peter Beardsley, although there are people who say he doesn't score enough goals. It just goes to show that you can't please all the people all the time, Peter! If Beardsley isn't scoring goals, someone in the side will be, make no mistake.

I have no doubt that in the long term both Ian Rush and Gary Lineker will benefit from having Beardsley alongside them. Both have gone through a lean patch for one reason or another. But that doesn't mean they've become bad players. Goalscorers will always go through bad spells. But players of the quality of Rush and Lineker will always get back among the goals eventually.

Sometimes you can judge the quality of a striker by the number of chances he misses. Yes, it sound silly . . . but no-one is going to score goals unless he gets himself into the right positions. It's no good hiding when things are going badly. I went through periods when I wondered if

I would ever get another goal. But I made sure I was still looking to score. Eventually the goals started to flow again. As someone once said, if you don't buy a raffle ticket, you won't win a prize.

If you want to know how good a striker is, just look at his record. Count the number of goals and the number of games and you'll soon see who the top men are. That's why I'll be watching the progress of young Steve Bull very closely. He looks the genuine article to me.

I saw him in action for Wolves against Bolton and he didn't seem to touch the ball more than about five times. But they included a header that was just off target, two shots that the keeper had to save, another shot that hit the post and a superb goal. Bull only knows one way to go . . . towards goal. Show him the whites of the post and he'll have a shot. We still have to see if he can score goals at the highest level. I think he will. Goalscorers are born and if a man can score 45 goals a season it doesn't matter if he's playing the girl guides every week. He's still got to be there to put the goals away. Lawton, Mortenson, Greaves, Lofthouse. We've all got the goals in the book. You can't take them away. And I'll stick my neck out and say Steve Bull will be up there, too, one day.

The 1966 World Cup win heralded the arrival of the all-purpose midfield player who has now become such a key figure throughout our game. I've been lucky at Bolton to have seen one of the very finest midfield players of the generation take his first steps along the road. I'm talking about Peter Reid.

Peter was always destined for the top but few players have overcome such barriers to get there. He suffered some horrendous injuries at Burnden Park but he never flinched in his determination to come back. Lesser men would have given up. Not Peter. And when he finally achieved his dream of a move into the big time with Everton, how he made it pay!

Peter is the kind of player every successful side must have. Hard but fair, he never gives up. He's a born winner but a gracious loser. He can win the ball and use it. Ask him to do a job and he'll do it. He's in the same mould as men like Billy Bremner, Dave Mackay and Eddie Colman. Few things in football have given me as much pleasure as his success for Everton and England and in the First Division. He has deserved every honour that has come his way.

Reid leads by example. Like Bryan Robson, surely one of the finest captains England have ever had. Bryan isn't just a great player; he's an inspiration to the men around him on and off the field. Have you ever heard anyone say a bad word about him? He never gives up. How many matches has he pulled out of the fire for Manchester United and England? There's no such thing as a lost cause with him around. His injury problems over the years have only served to show how vital he is for club and country. The old game can't be in such a bad way if it produces men like Bryan Robson.

CHAPTER SIXTEEN

My Italian Job

I TALKED earlier of my disappointing performance against Italy in Florence in 1952. The time they said Jackie Milburn should be flown out on a Comet to take my place for that fateful game against Austria in Vienna.

Well, I can't have been that bad against the Italians. Or let's put it this way . . . I must have impressed the locals. For later that year Bolton Wanderers received an offer for me from Fiorentina, the Italian First Division Club. Preston had a similar offer from another of the top Italian clubs for Tom Finney.

There was never much chance of me going. There was no freedom of contract in those days. If a player wanted to leave and his club said 'No', that was the end of the matter. There was no question of a player being a free agent at the end of his contract; there was no chance of a club cashing in on a prize asset before his contract expired.

If you hadn't signed on the dotted line by June 30 you were on a monthly contract until you did sign . . . or until the club decided to let you go. So Wanderers just told Fiorentina they were not prepared to sell me.

It didn't really worry me at the time. I was happy to play for Bolton. I was a regular first teamer in a successful side and England's first-choice centre-forward. My £14 a week doesn't sound much now but it was a reasonable amount at the time.

But, looking back, if there really had been a serious chance of me joining Fiorentina I would probably have gone. For a start they were offering me £60 a week. Big money. And then I always enjoyed playing against the Italians. I liked their style of play. Yes, they can be a bit volatile and they know all the tricks of the trade but basically the Italian First Division is a good place to play football.

They've always brought in the pick of the foreign players, so you're measuring your standards against the world's best every week. There is no doubt that nowadays with men like Maradona, Gullit, Van Basten and so many top South Americans, the Italian League is the best in the world. Those big games over there must have some atmosphere. Imagine playing in the San Siro Stadium in Milan or the Stadio Communale in Turin every other week. Big crowds, big-name players, big Soccer occasions. Wonderful!

Of course I never played in Europe. When we won the F.A. Cup in 1958 there was no Cupwinners Cup to enter the following season. By the time British clubs became regular competitors in the Cupwinners Cup and the old Fairs Cup I had long since departed the scene. A shame.

The first British player to really make it in Italy was John Charles, the Welsh giant who left Leeds United for Juventus in the mid-fifties. John was a superb player, equally at home in defence or attack. Very much like Duncan Edwards.

And he was an instant hit in Italy. He set his stall out to go over there, settle down with his family and succeed. He became the idol of the Italian fans, who always love anyone larger than life. Big John was certainly that. He was more than just a footballer. He was a cult figure.

I remember going on a family holiday to Portofino on the Italian Riviera in the late fifties. There were posters of John Charles everywhere. And wherever you went, those Welsh tones were booming out his hit record, Sixteen Tons. Yes, it was John Charles, pop star, too.

John realised as soon as he signed for Juventus that Italian football wasn't just a gravy train, a licence to print money. It meant hard work on and off the field. John had to make himself at home in a dressing room of complete strangers, some of whom may have resented the arrival of a highly-priced, highly-paid import.

He and his family had to adapt to the Italian way of life, to get used to the adulation of those fanatical fans . . . and the abuse when things went wrong. And above all, learn the language. You start with one hand tied behind your back if you can't even make yourself understood.

I'm sure that's the secret of a successful career on the Continent. It's no good going over and thinking you're on holiday, trying to take your own little piece of England to Italy, Spain or wherever. You have to go to become part of your new country. Make it your home.

Our next batch of Soccer exports to Italy were nothing like as successful as Big John. Jimmy Greaves went to AC Milan and Denis Law and Joe Baker to Torino. They were soon back home. The lifestyle of an Italian Soccer superstar was just not for them.

Gerry Hitchens, the old England centre-forward, fared much better in his spell with Inter Milan but it wasn't until the early eighties that we started exporting our stars in earnest again. Then there was quite a flood. Men like Joe Jordan, Liam Brady, Trevor Francis, Ray Wilkins, Mark Hateley and Graeme Souness became major figures in the Italian League. Kevin Keegan and Tony Woodcock played in Germany. Since then Gary Lineker has gone to Barcelona, Hateley, Glen Hoddle and Clive Allen to France and there are one or two more British players still active in a foreign field.

Good luck to them. I have nothing but admiration for players who are prepared to pull up their roots and really settle down in a foreign country. Yes, I know the rewards are high. But so is the casualty rate. Big names like Ian Rush and Mark Hughes were never able to come to terms with it irrespective of the money available.

But I've no doubt that the men who make a go of it in Europe return home much better players for the experience. How can you fail when you're coming up against world-class players week in and week out? And obviously the domestic players benefit, too. AC Milan's 1988 Championship-winning side is a case in point. They included their three world-class overseas players — Gullit, Van Basten and Rikjaard — but there was a hard core of Italians, too. Players who have developed into top-class stars through playing against the great international players every week. As they showed in their performances in the 1989 European Cup. Think what effect this has on the Italian national team. I for one would not bet against them in the 1990 World Cup Finals . . . to be played, of course, in Italy.

Since the ban on English clubs in Europe because of the Heysel Stadium disaster in 1985, our top players no longer compete against the best in the business. When the big clubs like Liverpool, Everton, Manchester United, Spurs and Arsenal were in Europe nearly every season, the pick of our players were in constant action against the top names from the rest of the world. It showed in their displays for the national side.

It's been noticeable that since the ban the English players have, on occasions, looked a bit naive. Some of the senior members of the side have, of course, got a fair bit of European experience. But the new boys and men just coming through have not. And it shows.

We have got good young players, make no mistake. But until they're competing against the top European sides regularly they will take a long time to develop their full potential at international level.

Arsenal's David Rocastle is a good example. He's a fine player, well worth his place in the England line-up. But it took him a long time to really show his true ability at international level. He's getting the feel of it now and will surely go on to become a key figure in the 1990s. But how much quicker he would have come through if Arsenal had been through to the last four of the UEFA Cup for the last three seasons.

Paul Gascoigne is another case in point. I think 'Gazza' has the makings of a major international star. He's strong, skilful and aware. A power player. I'm sure he would have done well in the European arena. But he hasn't had the chance. And this has held up his development as a full international player.

Another player who must surely become one of England's lynchpins in the '90s is Nigel Clough of Nottingham Forest. He is such a good little player; so clever, so intelligent. Like father, like son I suppose!

He's one of the best young players I've seen in years. He is capable of scoring 20 goals a season but you wouldn't really call him an out and out striker. He makes so many goals as well.

The performance which really pushed him into the public eye was in the 1989 League Cup Final against Luton Town. He scored two goals but, above all, he tore the Luton defence apart. Instead of playing up front, Clough came away 10 or 15 yards from the Luton defenders and said: 'Now, then, what are you going to do?'

If they came out to pick him up there was a gap at the back. If they stayed put, he was given all the time and space to create havoc. Which is just what he did. Yes, a clever player and a nice, clean-cut lad.

And while our exile from Europe has inevitably affected our leading players, top club sides and the international team, it has also taken so much of the traditional glamour out of our game. We've had some marvellous European nights, going right back to the fifties when Wolves played Honved of Hungary under that new phenomenon, floodlights. Marvellous tussles! I can still picture Johnny Hancocks and the rest on the old black and white screen. Then there were the Busby Babes and their memorable nights in the European Cup. They looked such certain winners until the tragedy of Munich.

Celtic took up the British standard with the famous Lions of Lisbon beating Inter Milan to land the European Cup in 1967, and from then until 1985 a season never seemed to pass by without an English side dominating one or other of the European competitions.

Who can forget Manchester United finally giving Matt Busby the European Cup in 1968? And at Wembley of all places. Or Bob Paisley's night of triumph with Liverpool in Rome? Cloughie's European Cup double? There were so many British sides who showed that our traditional strengths and style could still compete with the best at the very highest level.

Sadly Everton's Cupwinners Cup triumph over Rapid Vienna in Rotterdam in 1985 marked the end of an era. One day, surely, we will be back. That day can't come soon enough for me.

CHAPTER SEVENTEEN

A Family Affair

THEY say that behind every successful man there is a happy family. I've been lucky. I've got two . . . the people of Bolton and the Lofthouse family. I've always enjoyed a very special relationship with Bolton folk. I was born and bred in the town and I could never dream of living anywhere else. I've travelled all over the world and seen some marvellous sights. I've seen the beauty of Canada, the splendour of South Africa. I've been to North America and South America.

I've seen a lot of Europe, too, either playing football or as a tourist. But there's nothing to match those two lions outside Bolton Town Hall. That's the finest sight of them all. No matter where I go, it's nice to come home. This is where I belong.

But wherever I go there are always Boltonians to meet. It's amazing but I think there must be someone from Bolton in just about every corner of the world. Or that's how it seems, anyway.

My son Jeff has certainly discovered that. He lives and works overseas and when the names of Lofthouse and Bolton come into the conversation someone often turns round and says: 'Oh, I'm from Bolton, too. You're not related to Nat by any chance, are you?'

On my first trip abroad with the FA team to Canada it seemed that half of Bolton had emigrated there. I was always bumping into them. It's just the same today. And they never lose the accent.

An old pal of mine, Eddie Thornley, lives in Canada and a few years back he organised a dinner in Toronto in my honour. There were over 80 people from Bolton there, even the brother of the current groundsman at Burnden Park. It was a grand night.

But it was still good to be back home. People visiting Bolton after 20 years away always say how much the old place has changed. Of course it has. But it's still full of the same kind-hearted, good-natured people. They never change.

I always knew that when I went out to play for Bolton Wanderers I was representing the people of the town, too. I was a Boltonian and proud of it. I still am. I still want Wanderers to do well for the sake of the people who live in the town.

But however important the fans have been for me, I owe even more to my own family. It is absolutely vital for a footballer to have a happy, settled home life. I could never have gone away for eight weeks on a summer tour if I'd had the smallest worry about what was happening back home while I was away.

I suppose Alma must have known what to expect from the day we were married. That was on December 6, 1947. We were married at 11 o'clock in the morning and four hours later I was trotting out on to Burnden Park for a First Division match against Wolves.

We managed two or three days in Blackpool as a honeymoon but then it was business as usual in the number nine shirt for me. Or perhaps that's overstating it a bit. I was in the goals business, and between my wedding day and the end of the season I only hit the net a couple of times. You don't need me to go into detail about the kind of banter that came my way in the dressing room and on the terraces during that blank spell!

I had known Alma from the time we both went to Castle Hill School and, as I say, she knew from the start what was involved in being married to a professional footballer. This was not a nine to five office job or even a job down the pit with regular shifts. If I was successful I would be away for long spells in the summer. Away games would often involve overnight trips on a Friday, sometimes even staying on Saturday night, too.

And there's no such thing as Christmas celebrations for a professional footballer. In my day we often used to play on Christmas Day as well as Boxing Day. Easter too. That was just part of the job.

Alma accepted this and did everything she could to make sure we had a solid home life. I wouldn't have played well enough to be chosen for England if I'd had domestic worries at the back of my mind.

She wasn't a football fan before we got married but I don't think she ever missed at game at Burnden Park afterwards. She would bring the kids, Jeff and Viv, along — until Jeff started playing himself, of course — and they would meet up with the other players' families in a little room in the stand. The players would join them for a drink after the game.

I often wondered what it was like for Alma to hear the fans cheering or jeering me, but she never let it affect her either way. Sitting with all the other wives, I think she could afford to have a bit of a giggle about it. Bolton was always a family club — it always has been — and they would organise a coach for the wives to go along to important games away from home, too. Usually big Cup-ties.

Alma was in charge of my collection of caps, medals and trophies. She always kept them clean and tidy. She'd put them away for safe keeping in a box up in the rafters. In fact they're still there to this day.

She stood by me through the good times and the bad. She didn't particularly want to go into the pub venture at the Castle Hotel but joined in, knowing it might be vital for our future after my playing days were over.

She knew how much I needed her support during the difficult days when I was Manager. It can't have been much fun for her to sit in the stand and hear the fans calling for my head. But she never let me see if it was getting her down.

It wasn't easy for the kids at school, either. They were getting some stick because their Dad was Manager of Wanderers and Wanderers were doing badly. But Alma helped them through it.

She saw me through the dark days after I had been sacked as Chief Scout, and in a way I'm sure she was relieved that it was all over. But she shared my delight when Wanderers called me back into the fold.

From the start she wanted me to reach the top and was willing to sacrifice anything to help me get there. I would not be where I am today without her. When she died suffering from cancer in 1985, I was totally devastated. I will never get over it.

Of course I still see a lot of Jeff and Viv. In fact in the summer, I have a job making up my mind where to take Sunday lunch . . . Astley Bridge or Antibes! Viv lives in Astley Bridge here in Bolton. Jeff and his wife Michelle have an apartment in Antibes in the South of France. I'm a regular visitor to both.

Viv has been in the Police force for 12 years now. Like her Dad, she's a sports fanatic. She plays hockey, badminton, tennis. All sports, in fact. And there was a time when it looked as if Jeff might follow in his father's footsteps. He was a centre-half as a lad. A good player. I think he might have made it as a pro. But he never really wanted to.

I used to go along and watch him and hear all the comments like: 'You'll never be as good as your Dad.' It wasn't easy for him. I was glad he decided against it really, although Alma and I only ever wanted both of them to be happy in whatever they chose.

Jeff works for an international construction company. His work has taken them all over the world. I spend a lot of time at their apartment

Wounded Lion. That's me on the ground after scoring the winner against Austria. Jack Froggatt shouldn't be so worried — I was back in top form for the after-match celebrations.

Vienna, 1952. British troops lead the cheers for England.

Farewell to all that . . . my last Wembley appearance. England v Russia, October 22, 1958. I scored once in a 5-0 win.

Here I am with prized Soccer memorabilia. Pride of place goes to 'The Lion of Vienna'. Story on page 34.

You haven't changed at all! The 1958 side get together with more big names from Bolton's past at one of my Testimonial dinners. Back row (left to right): Roy Hartle, Bryan Edwards, Brian Birch, Me, George Taylor, Tommy Woodward, John Higgins, Tommy Banks, Dennis Stevens. Front: Ray Parry, Ralph Gubbins, Doug Holden and George Hunt.

DOWN YOUR WAY . . . Brian Johnston calls in at Burnden Park to interview me for his Radio Four series.

No hard feelings but . . . I share a joke with Blackpool's 1953 Wembley heroes Jackie Murdie (left) and Sir Stanley Matthews.

For the record . . . Folk group The Houghton Weavers join me to launch the record, 'The Lion of Vienna'.

Beating the drum for a Bolton bid to form the world's biggest brass band.

Every picture tells a story . . . this one was painted by former Bolton striker Paul Fletcher at the start of my testimonial year.

Smile please! Tom Finney joins in the fun at the start of my Testimonial Year.

1986 . . . Out come the Wembley souvenirs as Wanderers set off for the Freight Rover Trophy Final against Bristol City.

A couple of swells. With Tom Finney again at the publication of my Testimonial brochure.

At the launch of the Adult Training Scheme in Bolton, pictured with the scheme manager Ken Whowell.

In the swim . . . presenting a cheque to some local youngsters who raised over £500 for the Walk for Life charity . . . by swimming Lake Coniston and Lake Windermere.

during the summer. Sometimes they are away on their travels; sometimes they are there, too.

I've been all along the coast. Places like Cannes, Nice, Frejus, St. Tropez, Monte Carlo. One summer we made a sentimenal return trip into Italy. To Portofino where all those years ago we'd heard John Charles's record of Sixteen Tons.

Their apartment is just back off the seafront. I have a regular route for my morning stroll . . . down to the front in Juan les Pins, round the coast and up into old Antibes. I love to wander round the fish and fruit markets and along the old streets, stopping for a drink or a coffee. I've made a few friends over the years and usually bump into someone I know.

It's beautiful. If I time it right I'm just in time for a couple of beers before a bite to eat at one of the cafes near the harbour or in the old town. If Jeff and Michelle are there we'll probably meet for lunch.

Alternatively, there's a little train that runs right along the front and then through Antibes into the old town. I've always had a soft spot for little trains and it's often a strong temptation for the return journey back to the flat after a good lunch! It's garaged — if that's the word to use for a train! — right opposite Jeff's place.

In the evenings in Juan you can sit and have a meal and watch the pavement artists. They have jugglers, acrobats, fire eaters. All that sort of thing. I've been going for six or seven years now. It's something I really look forward to every time.

So if you're ever down on the Riviera and you think that chap on the little train in Antibes looks familiar, give me a shout. I'll buy you a beer!

CHAPTER EIGHTEEN

Hillsborough

April 16, 1989, should have been one of the happiest days of my 50 years in football. I was to be a guest of honour at the annual dinner of the Professional Footballers Association at the Hilton Hotel in London. The PFA dinner is a special night. It's the occasion when footballers everywhere gather to present their awards for the season. I was to receive a special merit award in recognition of my service to Bolton Wanderers and my 50 years in the game.

But the 1989 dinner was no night of celebration. There were tears not cheers. The previous day nearly 100 people had been crushed to death at the F.A. Cup semi-final between Liverpool and Nottingham Forest at Hillsborough. It was the blackest day in the history of our national game. No words of mine can express the horror we all felt as the tragedy unfolded before our eyes on television.

It should have been such a marvellous afternoon. A beautiful Spring day, two of the best sides in the country contesting the ultimate honour in the game, a place in the F.A. Cup Final at Wembley. There was magic in the air. But everything went tragically wrong.

We thought it could never happen again. After the 1946 disaster at Burnden Park in which 33 people lost their lives we thought our stadiums would be made safer places. But no. There followed the Ibrox disaster in 1971. The Bradford City fire in 1985. Then, soon afterwards, that terrible night at the Heysel Stadium in Brussels when fans went on the rampage before the Liverpool v Juventus European Cup Final. And now Hillsborough.

It's not for me to say what went wrong and why; to speculate on who was to blame. I can only say that Hillsborough 1989 must NEVER be repeated.

The scenes at Hillsborough brought back horrific memories for me of the Burnden Park disaster. That was on March 9, 1946. And there are so many similiarities between these two awful days, separated by 43 years.

Like Hillsborough, Burnden Park was the scene of an important Cup-tie — if any game of football can be called important when tragedies of this magnitude are involved. It was the sixth round of the F.A. Cup, Bolton Wanderers against Stoke City, a Stoke side that included the world's most famous footballer, Stanley Matthews.

It was a game everyone wanted to see. I have never seen Burnden Park so full. If you'd thrown a golf ball in the air it would have come down on someone's head. There was no space at all. Over 65,000 people had paid to get in and there was speculation later that something like 20,000 had got in without paying.

When we kicked off, police and ambulance men were lifting fans out of the crowd and there were people lying outside the touchline at the embankment end. I thought they had fainted. After about 15 minutes a police inspector ran on to the pitch and told the referee that he had to stop the game.

We went off. Stretcher cases were brought through the dressing rooms while we waited to restart but I don't think any of the 22 players on that field knew the extent of the disaster. Nor did the vast majority of the fans packed on to the terraces.

After a break of about 20 minutes the police chief asked the referee to restart the game. Communications were not so sophisticated in those days. It would not have been easy to let all those people know what had happened and why the game was being stopped.

I think he was worried about getting all the fans away if the game was abandoned without them knowing really what had happened. After all, if the players on the pitch didn't know the full horror of the situation, how could fans 100 yards away at the other end of the ground be expected to know?

The match ended in a goalless draw. It wasn't until afterwards that we learned people had been killed, one of them a woman. It was not until we read the papers the following day that the enormity of the tragedy was revealed. Thirty-three people had died as crush barriers collapsed under the sheer weight of numbers. Another 24 were in hospital. Over 500 had been treated at the ground.

I went back to the ground on the Sunday morning. It was a pitiful sight. There were shoes, ties, gloves, hats and other bits of clothing on the running track around the ground. We all felt so helpless.

How did it happen? There was a suggestion afterwards that a father and his small boy, frightened at the size of the crowd building up on the embankment, had forced open an exit door and escaped from the crush. In doing so they opened the floodgates for a tidal wave of people to surge into the ground.

That may or may not have been the case. But certainly the disaster was the result of people forcing their way on to the already overcrowded embankment.

I attended the inquest that was held soon afterwards. It seemed the least I could do. There was a memorial service. The Mayor of Bolton launched an appeal fund which raised over £40,000 for the families of the dead. We played a match against Hull City in aid of the fund.

The Home Secretary, Chewter Ede, announced an immediate inquiry, to be chaired by a King's Counsel, Moelwyn Hughes, to investigate the causes of the disaster. It concluded that there had been no structural failure, the tragedy had been caused by sheer weight of numbers.

Alterations were made to the embankment terracing at a cost of £5,500 and the inquiry called for all sports arenas to be inspected regularly for safety checks.

The town of Bolton was in a state of shock. It was less than a year since the end of the Second World War. Football was supposed to be one of the ways in which ordinary people could get away from the hardships and the sorrow that War had brought.

Now you see why Hillsborough, 1989, brought back so many painful memories for me. I was at a match at Bury on that fateful afternoon. When I saw those awful scenes on the television I thought immediately of Burnden Park, 1946.

I know how those people felt who had lost loved ones because I had seen Bolton people suffering in the same way. In 1946 there were no grief counselling services to help them recover. Everyone, friends and neighbours, rallied round to do their best. Just as the people of Liverpool did after Hillsborough.

I know, too, how the players felt. Of course they didn't want to play football again. On that Sunday morning when I learned the full horrors of the Burnden Park tragedy I felt just the same. John Barnes pulled out of an England World Cup match eleven days after the disaster. John Aldridge withdrew from the Republic of Ireland squad. Others felt they had come to terms with their grief and could start playing again.

But however terrible a tragedy, the world must go on. Eventually football had to start again, however recent the scars. That is what the people who died at Hillsborough would have wanted.

I am sure, too, that it was right to go ahead with the 1989 F.A. Cup Final as a memorial to the 95 who were killed. And how fitting that Liverpool should beat Forest to earn a Wembley final against their Merseyside friends and rivals, Everton.

Liverpool's first League match after the tragedy had been against Everton at Goodison Park, an occasion that once again showed how united the fans of Merseyside are.

And Wembley, the F.A. Cup Final, the world's greatest football match was the perfect memorial to the Hillsborough victims. The result was irrelevant. What mattered was that the red and blue sides of Liverpool, united in grief over Hillsborough, should be able to use the world's finest soccer stage as a tribute to the dead fans.

But now, with Hillsborough still fresh in our memories, it's time for the talking to stop. We need action. We must make our grounds safe places for people to go. Since 1946, we have learned a lot about how to make grounds safer . . . but no-one should have had to die in the process.

So what do we do? For a start, the fences must go. Those kiddies in the front rows at Hillsborough would be alive today if they had been able to escape on to the pitch. Yes, fans may run on to the field during a game if there are no fences. But that is a small risk set against the life of a child.

Didn't we learn ANYTHING from the Bradford City fire? Fifty-six people died. A terrible statistic. But if there had been fences around Valley Parade that day thousands more would have been burned to death. The only line of escape from the flames was on to the pitch and that is where the survivors went.

Then we must seriously consider all-seater stadiums; certainly at the big clubs who can expect large, near-capacity crowds week in and week out. When Coventry City tried to introduce an all-seater stadium some time ago the fans objected and the club climbed down.

Now we know the consequences of overcrowded terraces it's time to think again. In some ways it's a shame. I know people here at Bolton who have stood in the same spot on the terraces or in the paddock for 40 years. It's a regular meeting place every match. 'Same time, same place next week!' That kind of thing. And there are fans, many of them, who genuinely love to be in the middle of the swaying crowd behind one of the goals. That's the special atmosphere of the football match for them.

But we know now how lethal those vast standing areas can become. Lives come first. If we can save lives by having all-seater stadiums we must have them.

There is a move, too, for purpose-built stadiums away from the town centres. Fair enough. Many of our grounds are in urban areas and surrounded by narrow streets. Access is difficult. It's hard for the police to keep an eye on the fans.

All those years ago when I played against Spain at the Bernabeu Stadium in Madrid they had a 140,000-capacity, all-seater stadium with ample car parking. There were restaurants, swimming pools. It was a place the family could go for the day, not just a football match. If the Spaniards could do that in the early 1950s, surely we can do it now.

It is hardly a new idea. There has been talk for some time of building a super stadium in the Birmingham area where big matches like Cup semi-finals can be played. There has been talk of converting Odsal Stadium in Bradford into a luxury ground.

But that is all there has been . . . talk. After Hillsborough is it too much to expect some action?

And I make this appeal to football fans everywhere: NEVER go to an all-ticket match if you don't have a ticket. You are bound to cause problems of one sort or another.

It is hard to appreciate the impact of the Hillsborough disaster on the Liverpool players who endured a similar experience at Heysel. They thought they would never see anything like that again. Now they have.

It was a situation that gave us a new insight into the strength of character of their manager, Kenny Dalglish. As I've said earlier in the book, Dalglish has never been a man to show his private side in public. After Hillsborough his emotions were exposed for all to see. The real man was on show for the first time. It was clearly a harrowing experience for him but one that he handled with great dignity.

Nothing on earth will ever bring back those poor souls who perished. The money their relatives receive from the appeal fund can never compensate for their loss. It can only give them some help in making a fresh start.

But all of us — the government, the football authorities, you and me — owe it to the memory of those who died to spare no effort in making absolutely sure that those terrible scenes are never repeated on any football ground anywhere in the world.

CHAPTER NINETEEN

Fifty Not Out

Fifty years is a long time by any standards. I certainly never dreamed when I signed for Bolton Wanderers in September, 1939, that I'd still be here at Burnden Park half a century later. All I wanted to do then was to play for Bolton Wanderers. I suppose, in a way, everything that has come along on top of that has been the icing on the cake.

I've had some marvellous times and met some marvellous people on the way to my 50th anniversary. There have been bad days, there have been sad days. But looking back there isn't much I would have changed.

Think of the men I've played with and against. Those great figures from the distant past when I first signed on as a nervous 14-year-old. Taylor, Hunt, Westwood, Atkinson, Goslin, Rodwell, Woodward and the rest.

Then the men who took me on those two romantic roads to Wembley, first in 1953 and then in 1958. How we wore the white shirt of Bolton with pride! Fine individual players all linked together by one common bond. Bolton Wanderers.

And my England colleagues, Finney, Matthews, Mortenson, Wright, Ramsey. Big Duncan Edwards and his Manchester United team-mates who died at Munich, Tommy Taylor and Roger Byrne. Bobby Charlton, whose star was rising as I faded from the international scene.

And many, many more. Countless football people who have made me laugh a lot, cry a little and given me a lifetime of memories.

I think of the fans who have been my constant companions through those 50 years. Sometimes they have jeered me — and no doubt I deserved it when they did! — but usually it was their cheers and encouragement that kept me going.

I never stepped out on to a football pitch anywhere in the world without saying a silent 'Thank You' to those Bolton fans who made it all possible. The Burnden Park fans love a trier and that's what I've always been in the cause of Bolton Wanderers.

What's more they won't see the back of me just yet. Maybe I have completed 50 years with the club but I'm reckoning on being around here, helping the Wanderers in any capacity, for a while longer. Until the age of 70. At least!

I could never have dreamed about what football had in store for me back in September, 1939. Today, I don't have a crystal ball either. But what does the future hold? Where will our game be in the year 2039?

No doubt they will be telling us how much fitter and faster the players are than they were back in the 1980s. There will be new names in the hall of fame. And yes, there will be a latter-day Lofty pointing out that fitter and faster does not necessarily mean better. Good players will always be good players.

If I have a dream it is that while football can advance ON the field it can go back in time OFF the field.

Let's get rid of the hooligans. Let's cut out the bad language. Let's make our grounds safe places for the true fans to go with their families to watch a game of football.

Let's bring the women and children back into football grounds. Let's give them comfortable stadiums. Let's bring back the time when you only needed a handful of policemen to control a ground full of fans, people who had come to the match to enjoy themselves not to make trouble.

Let's go back to the days when the fans felt safe to wear their colours with pride; to cheer without fear; to share a joke and 'well done' with the opposition at the end of the day.

An impossible dream? Who knows. Football is a team game. Not just the clubs and the players . . . but the fans as well. Everybody, in fact, who cares about the game. If we all pull in the same direction, perhaps we can make that dream come true.

Come on, let's give it a try!

Index

Action replays 64.
Aldridge, John 90.
Allardyce, Sam 57.
Allchurch, Ivor 66.
Allen, Clive 81.
Allison, Malcolm 46, 48.
Armfield, Jimmy 57.
Atkinson, Jack 3, 5, 93.
Atkinson, Ron 51, 52, 53.

Baily, Eddie 33.
Baker, Joe 80.
Ball, Alan 52, 72, 74.
Ball, Johnny 10, 13.
Banks, Gordon 69, 74.
Banks, Jack 56.
Banks, Ralph 5, 10, 13.
Banks, Tommy 18, 20, 22, 36, 68.
Barass, Matt 5, 10, 13.
Barnes, John 76, 90.
Bartram, Sam 30, 69.
Bassett, Dave 54.
Beardsley, Peter 67, 76.
Bell, Colin 46.
Bell, Eric 10, 13, 14.
Bentley, Roy 25, 35.
Best, George 50, 75, 76.
Birch, Brian 19, 20.
Bond, John 51, 52.
Booking (only one in career) 62.
Bradford City fire 88, 91.
Brady, Liam 81.
Bremner, Billy 76, 77.
Broadbent, Peter 20.
Brown, Mick 53.
Bull, Steve 77.
Burnden Park tragedy, 1946 88-91.
Busby, Sir Matt 16, 18, 22, 49-51, 75, 82.
Byrne, Roger 16-18, 93.

Canada F.A. tour 1950 23, 24.
Cantello, Len 57.
Carey, Johnny 16, 50.
Catterall, George 4.
Chadwick, Cliff 5.
Charles, John 66, 80, 87.
Charlton, Bobby 17, 18, 20, 21, 50, 74-76, 93.
Charlton, Jack 74.
Clarke, Alan 76.
Clayton, Ron 20.
Clemence, Ray 69.
Clement, Dave 57.
Clough, Brian 50, 51, 57, 83.
Clough, Nigel 50, 51, 82.
Cockburn, Henry 16.
Cohen, George 73, 74.
Cole, Bert 2.
Colman, Eddie 17, 18, 77.
Cooper, Terry 73.
Cope, Ron 20.
Crerand, Pat 75.
Crowd trouble 64-66.
Crowther, Stan 18, 20.
Cullis, Stan 19, 27.
Cunningham, Willie 38, 40.
Currie, Tony 57.
Currier, Jimmy 3.

Dalglish, Kenny 53, 54, 76, 92.
Davies, Alf 58, 59.
Dawson, Alex 18, 20.
Dickinson, Jimmy 30.
Ditchburn, Ted 30.
Dobing, Peter 20.
Docherty, Tommy 19, 40.
Douglas, Bryan 20.

Earlestown FC Supporters Club 34.
Eckersley, Bill 30.

Edwards, Bryan 19, 20.
Edwards, Duncan 16-18, 80, 93.
Ellis, Arthur 37, 64.
England v Austria, Wembley 1952 27, 28, 41.
England v Austria, Vienna 1952 31-34.
England v Finland, Helsinki 1956 41.
England v France, Highbury 1951 41.
England v Hungary, Budapest 1954 42.
England v Hungary, Wembley 1953 41.
England v Italy, Florence 1952 32.
England v Northern Ireland, Goodison 1953 42.
England v Rest of World, Wembley 1953 41.
England v Scotland, Wembley 1955 39.
England v Scotland, Hampden Park 1956 40, 41.
England v Spain, Madrid 1955 35.
England v USSR, Wembley 1958 41.
England v Wales, Villa Park 1958 41.
England v Yugoslavia, Highbury 1950 25, 41.
Entwhistle, Jim, Bolton mayor 3.
Evans, Roy 53.
Ewing, Dave 27, 36.

Garrett, Tommy 13.
Gascoigne, Paul 52.
Geldard, Albert 4.
Giles, Johnny 76.
Goodwin, Freddie 20.
Goslin, Harry 3-5, 93.
Gradi, Dario 54.
Graham, Arthur 57.
Gray, Eddie 76.
Greaves, Ian 18, 20, 57.
Greaves, Jimmy 49, 57, 74, 77, 80.
Greaves, Roy 57.
Gregg, Harry 17-21.
Grobbelaar, Bruce 68.
Gubbins, Ralph 20.
Gullit, Ruud 80. 81.

Haddock, Harry 40.
Hagan, Jimmy 23.
Hamlett, Lol 5.
Hancocks, Johnny 20, 23, 29, 82.
Hankin, Ray 57.
Hanson, Stan 4, 5, 10, 13, 23.
Hart, Paul 57.
Hartle, Roy 18, 20, 36.
Hassall, Harold 10, 13, 14.
Hateley, Mark 80, 81.
Hennin, Derek 19, 20.
Heysel Stadium disaster 72, 81, 88.
Hidegkuti, Nandor 42.
Higgins, John 19, 20.
Hillsborough disaster 88-92.
Hitchens, Gerry 81.
Hoddle, Glenn 81.
Hodgkinson, Alan 69.
Holden, Duggie 10, 13, 14, 18-20.
Hopkinson, Eddie 18, 20, 21, 69.
Howe, Don 4, 5.
Hughes, Billy 10.
Hughes, Mark 81.
Hunt, George 3, 5, 48, 93.
Hunt, Roger 49, 74.
Hurley, Charlie 49.
Hurst, Geoff 74, 75.
Hurst, Jack 4.

ID cards 66.
Ithell, Jack 4, 5.

Johnston, Harry 13, 15.
Jones, Mark 17, 18.
Jones, Paul 57.
Jones, Vinny 64.
Jordan, Joe 81.

Langton, Bobby 10, 13, 14, 29.
Law, Denis 50, 75, 76, 80.
Lawton, Tommy 2, 7, 16, 24, 77.
Lee, Francis 45, 46.
Lifeline scheme 58, 59.
Lineker, Gary 76, 81.
Lofthouse, Alma (Nat's wife) 25, 32, 43, 44, 49, 85, 86.
Lofthouse, Dick (Nat's brother) 1.
Lofthouse, Edward (Nat's brother) 1.
Lofthouse, Jeff (Nat's son) 25, 84-87.
Lofthouse, Michelle (Nat's daughter-in-law) 86, 87.
Lofthouse, Richard (Nat's father) 1, 25.
Lofthouse, Sarah Jane (Nat's mother) 1.
Lofthouse, Tom (Nat's brother) 1, 2.
Lofthouse, Viv (Nat's daughter) 85, 86.

Manning, John 49.
Maradona, Diego 80.
Matthews, Reg 17.
Matthews, Sir Stanley 7, 11, 12-15, 23, 26, 28, 29, 30, 35, 39, 40, 72, 89, 93.

Maximum wage 67, 68.
Meadows, Jimmy 58.
Medley, Les 29.
Mercer, Joe 46, 48.
Merrick, Gil 30, 33, 69.
Midgley, Neil 64.
Milburn, Jackie 17, 24, 29, 32, 79.
Moir, Willie 5, 10, 13.
Moore, Bobby 74.
Moran, Ronnie 53.
Morris, Johnny 16.
Mortenson, Stanley 13-15, 17, 24, 41, 60, 68, 77, 93.
Mudie, Jackie 13.
Mullen, Jimmy 20, 29, 37.
Munich air crash 16-18, 41, 44, 82.
Murphy, Jimmy 18-22.
Musil, Austrian goalkeeper 1952 33.

Mackay, Dave 77.
McAdams, Billy 45, 71.
McIlroy, Jimmy 56.
McMenemy, Lawrie 51, 51.

Nicholson, Billy 51, 53.
Northern Ireland 39-42.

Ocwirk, Ernst 31, 32.

Paisley, Bob 53, 82.
Parry, Ray 19, 20.
Pearson, Mark 18.
Pearson, Stanley 40, 50.
Pegg, David 17, 18.
Pele 6.
Perry, Bill 13, 15.
Peters, Martin 72, 74.
PFA award 1989 88.
Platini, Michel 10.
President, Bolton Wanderers FC 59, 65.
Prince Philip 21.
Pub managing 18, 43, 44.
Puskas, Ferenc 10, 42.
Pye, Jesse 20, 25.

Queen Elizabeth II 11, 12.

Ramsey, Alf 27, 28, 41, 48, 72, 73, 93.
Referees 37, 62-65.
Reid, Peter 57, 77.
Retirement 46, 47.
Revie, Don 40, 53, 57, 76.
Richards, Sir Gordon 11.
Ridding, Bill 6, 48.
Rikjaard, Frank 81.
Roberts, Jack 4.
Robinson, Cyril 13.
Robson, Bobby 26, 27.
Robson, Bryan 53, 77, 78.
Rocastle, David 81.
Rodwell, Teddy 3, 93.
Rose, Henry 44.
Rowley, Jack 16, 25, 50.
Rush, Ian 76, 81.

Schools 1-3, 85.
Scotland, in 1954 World Cup 38.
Scotland, playing against 39-41.
Sewell, Jackie 23, 32.
Shackleton, Len 68.
Shankly, Bill 4, 5, 53, 76.
Sherpa Van Trophy 60, 61.
Shilton, Peter 69.
Shimwell, Eddie 13.
Siddall, Barry 57.
Signing for Bolton 3.
Sinclair, Tommy 4.
Slater, Bill 20.
Souness, Graeme 76, 80.
South of France (holidays) 86, 87.
Southall, Neville 70.
Springett, Ron 69.
Stevens, Denis 19-21.
Stiles, Nobby 22, 74, 75.
Summerbee, Mike 46.
Swift, Frank 44, 69.

Taylor, Ernie 13-15, 18.
Taylor, George 3, 5, 6, 7, 19, 25, 48, 93.
Taylor, Gordon 46.
Taylor, Graham 54.
Taylor, Tommy 16-18, 20, 37, 41, 93.
Thornley, Eddie 84.
Trautman, Bert 69.
Trotter, Jimmy 33, 73.

Van Basten, Marco 80, 81.
Venables, Terry 51, 52.
Violett, Dennis 17, 20.

Waddle, Chris 67.
Wages 8, 25, 67.
Wales 39-41.
War, outbreak of Second World War 3.
Warburton, Derek 58.
Ward, Tim 33.
Wartime soccer 4, 5.

Webster, Colin 20.
Wedding to Alma 85.
Westwood, Ray 2-5, 93.
Whatmore, Neil 57.
Wheeler, Johnny 10, 13.
Wilkins, Ray 81.
Williams, Bert 20, 30, 33, 69.
Wilshaw, Dennis 37, 40.
Wilson, Ray 74.
Winter, Danny 4, 5.
Winterbottom, Walter 26, 36, 48, 49, 70.
Woodburn, Willie 40.
Woodcock, Tony 81.
Woodward, Tommy 3, 93.
Work — in mill, down mines 3.
World Cup 1954, Switzerland 37, 38.
World Cup 1966, England 28, 72-75.

Young, George 40.

Zemen, Austrian goalkeeper 1952 28.